LIVING BENEATH THE COLORADO PEAKS

THE STORY OF KNAPP RANCH

A Vision of Architectural Design
and Land Stewardship

LIVING BENEATH THE COLORADO PEAKS

THE STORY OF KNAPP RANCH

A Vision of Architectural Design and Land Stewardship

Betsy and Bud Knapp

With Sarah Chase Shaw

Featuring the photography of Todd Winslow Pierce

Foreword by Kim Langmaid

THE KNAPP PRESS

For Betsy Wood Knapp
March 3, 1943 – June 20, 2017

Gracious, Innovative, Playful,
Generous, Entrepreneurial, Authentic

CONTENTS

Tucked in the shadow of ancient mountains, Colorado's Knapp Ranch is nestled amid a dramatic Western landscape. Both solitude and adventure can be found in this Rocky Mountain valley, occasionally heightened by the hint of danger that comes with the prospect of a genuine encounter with the wild. It is a place that encourages both visitors and longtime residents to respond with awareness and respect.

Craftsmanship, authenticity and tradition took center stage as the building compound began to take shape. In his essay, Austrian master wood craftsman Rudi Neumayr praises the art of woodworking, suggesting that craftsmanship can help encourage and establish sustainability for the future.

A gallery of images and accompanying text reveal the influence of the surrounding natural environment, the region's unique history and the use of National Park Service rustic—sometimes called "Parkitecture"—on the interior finishes and unique details found in the architecture, interior design, and landscape architecture.

FOREWORD

KIM LANGMAID

Reciprocity

The upper West Lake Creek Valley is a cradle carved by a glacier and circled by mountains. You enter the valley over a great moraine—a tall arc of sand and rocks, a final gift left behind by the ice. A winding dirt road approaches the valley, climbing through a forest of pine, spruce, and aspen. Scattered across the landscape you can see glacial erratics—huge boulders plucked from the bedrock, colored with swirls of minerals, polished and then relinquished as relics of the glacial past. When you crest the moraine, you know you've arrived. Like a great natural amphitheater, the valley unfolds before you. Your gaze is drawn irresistibly across a great trough of beauty until it finally rises and settles in awe on the high mountains.

Every summer for almost two decades, I've made a pilgrimage to this valley. Most times I go there to teach and learn with a group of other educators. But sometimes I go there alone. When I'm by myself, I stand at the top of the moraine and soak in the energy that emanates from the peaks. I'm not the only one who's come here like this, to learn from the mountains, and receive the inspiration and sustenance that flow through wind, water, stone, and blood.

Someone once told me there is a medicine wheel close by—a sacred place where Ute Indians gathered to pay their respects and celebrate the summer solstice. The Ute came here to honor the sun and give thanks for the high country's bounty of elk, deer, bear, and bighorn sheep. The Ute, who call themselves "the mountain people," carry out rituals of stewardship through the seasons. Anthropologists say that, for approximately ten thousand years, the Ute circled through the Colorado mountains, traveling on foot in a sun-wise direction. They arrived at each place, at exactly the right time, to fulfill their annual ancestral obligation to demonstrate their gratitude for the mountains.

I, too, see this valley as a gift. Each time I visit, I walk its contours and listen for what wants to be learned. At first, the lessons I received were fairly straightforward: the complex, interconnected facts of natural history, geology, and ecology. Later, I looked at the land through the lens of an artist, searching for the patterns, colors, and textures that weave themselves together to make a place that is beautiful and whole. Now, in these days of climate change and uncertainty, the questions are more complicated: How does a person nurture those deeper yearnings of the land—conservation, evolution, and adaptation to rapid environmental change? How does an educator cultivate the kind of curiosity and compassion that inspires essential new visions of sustainable communities?

One morning, while teaching a group of people about birds, I saw something bizarre and unexpected in that valley: A flock of white-faced ibis migrating in precise formation over the meadows, moving in a direction I thought they shouldn't go. The birds were clearly off course, I thought. But the gangly group kept going, flying toward the stark gray precipice of the peaks and finally disappearing over the cold mountains. Later that day, however, those birds surprised me, and I suddenly realized that they knew exactly what they were doing. On my way home, I realized the ibis had flown in a great loop. I found them way down low near the valley creek's confluence with the river, mucking around, contentedly probing with their curled bills and gorging on insects in a muddy irrigated field. Perhaps they had sought the stillness of the morning skies for their own kind of ritual journey.

Property owners Bud and Betsy Knapp moved to the valley in the 1990s. They thoughtfully and carefully took their time to settle in. First, they studied the language of the land; then they built a welcoming home and cozy gathering place, with beautiful bookshelves crafted from beetle-killed pine trees harvested from the surrounding forest. They have a powerful vision for conservation. They've decided to nurture the valley for themselves and future generations. They invite educators like me to bring our questions, and our passions, and to use the valley as a learning laboratory—enhancing our connection to nature and inspiring provocative ideas in ecology, education, and sustainable living.

The Knapps undid the decades of damage that earlier settlers and unrestrained livestock had inflicted on the creek and riparian habitat. Now healed, the creek water playfully skips through the valley, dipping into deep rocky pools and bubbling up with the earthy understated sweetness of life in the high mountain West. Freshly planted, high-elevation experimental vegetable gardens soak up the short summer sun and feed the Knapps and their extended family and friends. Blankets of wildflowers bloom here—white geranium, scarlet gilia, purple penstemon, golden aster, and bouquets of blue columbine—creating a brilliant quilt that welcomes all kinds of native pollinators. Jewel-colored migratory hummingbirds buzz and hover, back and forth, around and through the meadows, seeking nectar and delivering grains of precious pollen to perpetuate life.

I think there's a pattern and progression that happens when you strive to know a place well. At first, you want to know the names of things and how they're all connected. You search for the flickers that spark your curiosity. Then there is a slower learning process. You peel away layers and discover the land's deeper meanings. You crave intimacy, the caress of this special sense of place.

Places like this valley cultivate our innate sense of reciprocity—the most basic form of gift exchange. Lewis Hyde, author of the book *The Gift*, says, "When we see that we are actors in natural cycles, we understand that what nature gives to us is influenced by what we give to nature. So the circle is a sign of an ecological insight as much as of gift exchange." The root words of reciprocity are *re* and *pro*, meaning *back* and *forth*. Our acts of education, conservation and stewardship are not acts of charity; they are acts of reciprocity.

These days, when I visit the valley, I feel this sense of reciprocity. I see the gifts of snow and clean water flowing to the Colorado River. I smell the awakening scents of sagebrush and subalpine fir trees. I listen to the gentle tapping of hungry nuthatches and the quaking leaves of aspen trees. I taste wild strawberries and touch the cool glacial erratics. And I am moved by gratitude.

In the end, it's places like this little valley that care for us. We think we're good stewards of the land, conserving species and restoring forests and watersheds, but these places sustain us in more than material ways. Places like this little valley cradle and nurture our humanity; they keep us creative and resilient. They replenish the forgotten depths of our human nature. Even when we can't be there in person, these special places come and go in our hearts, circling back like migratory birds, hovering in our memories, bringing gifts of beauty, hope and creativity, and inspiring new visions for sustainable communities.

—Kim Langmaid, Ph.D.
Founder, Vice President, and Director of Sustainability and Stewardship Programs at Walking Mountains Science Center in Avon, Colorado.

PROLOGUE
BETSY AND BUD KNAPP

Acting on a Dream

When we began building our home in Colorado, writing a book documenting the process was the last thing on our minds. Entrepreneurs at heart, we love process; we enjoy reading plans, we can remember tiny details, and we have the ability to visualize results. Never once did it occur to us that our process might be of any interest to others. It was at the topping-off party, a celebration for everyone who had participated in the design and construction of our home, that it finally dawned on us that we needed to memorialize the process, the people, and the place.

Living Beneath the Colorado Peaks began simply as a way to provide insight into our approach—by way of video, photography, drawings and other pertinent information—for our friends and family, and also as a chance to acknowledge the talented people who helped create the place. Friends, family, even total strangers wanted to know what we did and how we did it. Most importantly, however, they wanted to know why. This last part puzzled us. What was it about our project that had piqued the interest of so many people—enough to get us to think twice about producing a book? Finally, it hit us that our story is interesting because we acted on a dream. It's the same dream that many people have at some point in their lives, but it had a more specific purpose that was guided by our interest in architecture, history and place.

For many years, we published *Architectural Digest*, and we spent a lot of time shuttling between coasts, living and working in Boston, New York, Chicago, and Los Angeles. During that time, we were lucky enough to share a condominium in Vail with our good friends, Alison and Kurt Burghardt. The condominium's windows looked out over a lively tourist scene that had been built around the beauty of an extraordinary natural setting. Even then, we knew that we needed to make a change in our lifestyle; we were determined to find a way to live more permanently in this part of the world. We turned our sights toward finding a property where we could surround ourselves with those things we really value: open space, independence, and privacy.

In the early 1990s, we discovered that place in a high mountain valley just west of Vail. We began the process of creating a new home, one that combined some of the creative elements of our previous life with the natural beauty and historic character of this new environment.

In *Living Beneath the Colorado Peaks*, we share the adventure of creativity and what it means to build something that has personality and meaning. Certainly, this book is about the process of design and construction, as well as about the inspiration we derived from the place and the people. But more importantly, it's a story about what it means to create a unique project in a remote setting like this, where true knowledge and appreciation of the special surrounding environment are paramount to constructing a home that looks, feels, and lives like it truly belongs there.

During the design and construction process, we challenged everyone working on the project—from architects and designers, to craftspeople and artisans, to builders and tradesmen—to think outside the box by asking them to envision themselves as nineteenth-century settlers in the valley. We gave them free rein to explore their ideas and make use of their skills, and in return, we asked them to give us their best possible work. This was an opportunity, we said, to show off their creativity and share their craft. Many had become accustomed to the commercialism inherent in their trade, something that has become ubiquitous in resort communities around the world. It took a lot of faith and perseverance to give them the confidence to return to the basics of their craft, and to produce the most beautiful things they could make by hand.

When they saw how much we admired and appreciated their work, their pride and delight was contagious. Knowing of our history in the publishing business, many of those artists and designers asked if we were going to produce a book. Similarly, guests inspired by the size of the stone used in the mantle in Marmot Lodge, and intrigued by the swinging bed on the porch at Anglers Cabin, or refreshed by a walk around the lake, wanted to know more about the area and its history. "There must be a story to this place," they would say. Why did we build a series of log cabins that look like they have been here for over a hundred years? Where did we find the artists and craftspeople to do such excellent work in such an authentic way? How did we develop an interest in agriculture and in growing our own food? And finally: How are we managing this land to help it retain its beauty and biodiversity? The answer to almost every question begins, quite simply, with our love of the land.

In 2013, we moved permanently to the upper West Lake Creek Valley, trading the convenience and cultural advantages of Los Angeles for the privacy and peace of central Colorado. Solitude, however enticing, brings with it a host of challenges that keep us constantly on our toes, and our days are spent quite differently now that we live in a remote mountain valley. When it snows, we have to dig ourselves out. When the temperatures dip below zero, the pipes can freeze. Internet and cell phone service are intermittent luxuries obtainable only from the highest ridges surrounding the ranch. Our most frequent visitors have four legs, not two. Raising honeybees, milling logs, and growing vegetables are activities that we had always applauded others for doing; now, in an effort to be sustainable, we have become beekeepers, farmers, and foresters. And instead of watching the television, we watch the weather, gauging our own cyclic rhythms by the seasonal changes we observe around us. We are building a base of knowledge with the help of innumerable experts. And so this book is our way of sharing that knowledge with the hope that others may benefit from the many lessons we learned along the way.

"Sacred land" is a phrase used frequently these days, both by Native Americans trying to protect land and by non-Natives sensitive to the cause. For us, the term implies a shared spiritual reality that transcends beauty. From the moment we crested the hill and saw this valley for the very first time, we have been enthralled by the beauty and openness of the land, and the rich variety of life that it sustains. What we built here and how we treat it is a testament to that gratitude. It is our hope that through this book and by our actions, we can convince others of the importance of protecting this natural treasure, and others like it. Welcome to our dream. —Betsy and Bud Knapp

Knapp Ranch Archives

This telephone, secured in a box and attached to a post in the middle of the job site, became the project's unofficial conference room. Despite the constant noise and dust, the Knapps conducted all of their business, both personal and professional, from this station throughout the four-year building project. Needless to say, they missed a lot of incoming calls!

INTRODUCTION
SARAH CHASE SHAW

A Book for Information and Inspiration

Living Beneath the Colorado Peaks is as much an exposition of ideas and process as it is a tribute to the place. The story, one that began over three decades ago, continues to evolve, its premise and characters changing with new discoveries and outcomes. Words and images can describe what has been created here, but the real story lies in the evolution of the place. What began as an adventure in designing and building a home together in the mountains of Colorado has become so much more, evolving into a complex and challenging journey into the heart of what it means to find personal fulfillment by living in nature.

When you are in the business of presenting beautiful design as a major component of an accomplished lifestyle, as the Knapps were for over 40 years, you tend to look at design through the lens of location. Cultural and physical geography, topography, people and place—all these are essential to any discussion of architecture. Collections of regional, historic, and culturally significant artifacts are often displayed as art, and practical furnishings that are suited to the setting are essential to creating a truly livable environment. In addition to location, loyalty to a certain level of quality ensures that the design has traction and will prove sustainable well into the future. As the publishers of *Architectural Digest*, *Bon Appétit* and a host of lifestyle-oriented coffee-table books, the Knapps had become adept at empowering experts, including designers, craftspeople, or purveyors of specialty products, to share the secrets of their success in order for readers the world over to step away from any page feeling inspired to create a project of their own—regardless of scale. The stories often brought out the implications of the setting, and its influence on lifestyle, and the importance of the choice of location in defining an overall point of view about authenticity and quality. This was a business model that the Knapps could, and did, translate directly to the design and construction of their home, and to the development of the agricultural and wood-product enterprises that now exist on the property. Using the orchard as an example, Bud Knapp describes the patience required to see the long-term benefits of such an endeavor. "At nine thousand feet, apples, pears and plums don't grow overnight. We believe that quality products, be they entrepreneurial start-up businesses, orchards, or building a home, take time. Through this book, we are able to show the importance of investing the time and necessary resources into developing and maintaining a vision for the future."

The purpose of *Living Beneath the Colorado Peaks* is to inspire you to create your own personal environment regardless of budget, location, or circumstance. The story you're about to read illustrates one way to accomplish this, but it's not the only way. The stunning imagery you see highlighted within these pages points to a natural environment of beauty and serenity that no human being could ever create, and it is a landscape that could easily be destroyed without proper respect and care. Places like these feed our souls, engage our minds and nourish our bodies, and now, more than ever, it is imperative that we do our part to preserve them for the future by carefully considering the footprints we leave behind. This is true whether your planned home is in a suburban neighborhood, a big city, a small town, or a remote mountain valley.

As you page through this book, take time to think about your own aspirations. How can you adapt what you see and what you read to your own circumstances? What kind of a footprint will you leave behind? *Living Beneath the Colorado Peaks* is not a best-practices manual, nor is it a primer on responsible design, building, and land management. It is simply a figurative model of one couple's dream.

In these pages, you will meet many real people—experts in their fields—whose talent and imagination form the backbone of their life's work. They include an architect best known for cultivating an inspired European design ethic in Vail; an interior design team dedicated to environmentally friendly furnishings and finishes; landscape architects whose environmental sensitivity ensured that this project would stand the test of time; a builder whose roots in these mountains are generations deep; a team of loggers whose love for, and knowledge of, the tools of their trade are clearly visible in the impeccable craftsmanship and details found throughout each cabin; stonemasons whose collective creativity is visible in the elegant simplicity of the stonework; an Austrian woodworker whose devotion to his craft is apparent in the interior details found throughout the main lodge and cabins; and a design team whose collective creativity can be seen in the compound of buildings where integrity and historic relevancy are integral to the genuine and authentic relationship the Knapps maintain with the surrounding landscape.

The book is divided into six chapters. The first sets the stage by describing the rich diversity of life that exists in the immense physical landscape surrounding Knapp Ranch. The challenges inherent in settling this rough and rocky environment become apparent in chapter two, which begins with a brief history of the area and a few of the characters who left indelible marks on this landscape. With the arrival of the Knapps in 1990, a vision for accommodating a home, or a compound of buildings, begins to emerge. The following three chapters are devoted to the design and construction of the Main Lodge and cabins. Authenticity and craftsmanship take center stage as local craftspeople engage in creating a building compound that accurately reflects the settlement history of the upper West Lake Creek Valley. Throughout these chapters, craftspeople describe the challenges involved in utilizing traditional construction techniques to create structures that are built to last a century or more. Photographs and sketches highlight such details as log joinery, window bucks, screw joints, and other historically accurate elements that are incorporated throughout the buildings found at Knapp Ranch. Chapter five is devoted to a gallery of images and text that describe the interior finishes and unique details found in each of the property's cabins and lodges. Chapter six marks a change in focus as the Knapps begin to explore the land through the lens of sustainable agriculture and preservation. A close look at the impacts of climate change on the mountain ecosystem leads to a thoughtful discussion of the local efforts being undertaken to combat them. The Knapps describe their desire to grow their own food and the challenges inherent in undertaking such an operation at nine thousand feet above sea level. *Living Beneath the Colorado Peaks* concludes with a plan for the future of Knapp Ranch that envisions the property as a hub of opportunity for the kind of idea generation, problem solving, learning and research that can be used by think tanks, institutions and mission-led organizations. At the same time, the ranch will continue to honor the Knapps' long-term vision through investments in education, sustainable agriculture, and place-based learning.

Within these pages, you may encounter terminology and concepts that are very specific to this project and to the Western landscape in which it is located. A great deal of information already exists on these subjects. But should you want to know more about topics ranging from sudden aspen decline to creating a productive fishery, sidebars have been included to clarify ideas in ways that will satisfy your curiosity, and maybe even pique your interest to know more. In addition, sprinkled throughout the book are essays and words of wisdom from some of the many talented individuals who contributed to this project, expressing the ideas and concepts that were integral to the success of Knapp Ranch.

This is first and foremost a story about the creation of one couple's dream home in a beautiful place, but it's also a story about many other people—all of them observing, learning, listening, engaging, and sharing in the joy of creation. People care what happens here because it's a place of opportunity and hope in a world of uncertainty. There is immense pleasure to be found in simply discovering for yourself what it means to find a place of infinite beauty, a place that satisfies your mind, body and spirit, a place that you can call home.

—Sarah Chase Shaw

When we first saw this valley, we were high atop a neighboring ridge, overlooking a panorama of valleys and mountains, forested slopes, and rocky peaks. The wildness and solitude of this seemingly uncharted area intrigued us because, when you're down in a valley, you don't have the perspective of space. Once we saw what was around us, our curiosity was piqued. We knew many hardy souls had been here before, but for us, this was new territory. —Betsy and Bud Knapp

1

OBSERVATION

UNDERSTANDING THE BEAUTY AROUND US

Preceding Spread: An overview of the Lake Creek region as seen from a nearby ridge on a summer evening: East Lake Creek Valley at far left, and West Lake Creek Valley below the peaks of the Sawatch Range at right. It was from a similar vantage point that the Knapps saw, for the first time, the immensity of the landscape and began to think about how they might find their own place within it.

Above: A granite monolith glows in the early morning light like the ruins of an ancient temple. Rugged formations such as this one near the summit of New York Mountain, directly south of Knapp Ranch, are the result of eons of weathering, erosion, and geologic upheaval. Moisture accelerates the process, seeping into cracks where it freezes, thaws, and cleaves the stone apart into a myriad of shapes and sizes.

A Wild and Varied Mountain Landscape

At the peak of the last glaciation about thirty-two thousand to fifteen thousand years ago, temperatures in the area we now call Colorado were approximately 7 to 11 degrees Fahrenheit colder than they are today, as ice sheets the size of continents covered northern North America and Eurasia. Above the site of today's Knapp Ranch, a large alpine glacier, fed by massive snowfall and cold temperatures, flowed from cirques surrounding New York Mountain, moving slowly to the north, cutting, grinding and chiseling its way through the surrounding landscape. At a point just below what is now the northernmost boundary of the ranch, the glacier stopped, depositing a mass of boulders, gravel, and sand in a semicircular form called a terminal moraine. When global temperatures increased due to enhanced solar radiation, the ice began to retreat, leaving behind huge, isolated rocks called glacial erratics, and an open valley defined on either side by steep slopes and bisected by a perennially flowing mountain stream. In the newly barren glacial landscape, lichens slowly formed, followed eventually by soil and then vegetation, gradually transforming the landscape into what is now the West Lake Creek Valley.

This valley is in the heart of Colorado's Rocky Mountains, fifteen miles west of Vail Ski Resort. Though access to it is straightforward, it is far enough removed from the valley floor to warrant a certain level of perseverance and curiosity. The path to this place starts in the undulating contours of the meandering Eagle River Valley some eighteen hundred feet below it, passing scattered homesites and open meadows edged by rail fences, tracing West Lake Creek through narrow draws to the point where it temporarily separates itself to ascend through aspen groves, thick with wildflowers—columbine, larkspur, and lupine—and teeming with wildlife. At the crest of the hill, the trees give way to the stunning vista of a private valley protected by a rim of jagged mountains. The first view of the valley is unforgettable.

When I was standing on the highest mountain of them all, and round about beneath me was the whole hoop of the world. And while I stood there I saw more than I can tell and I understood more than I saw; for I was seeing in a sacred manner the shapes of all things in the spirit, and the shape of all shapes as they must live together like one being. And I saw that the sacred hoop of my people was one of many hoops that made one circle, wide as daylight and as starlight, and in the center grew one mighty flowering tree to shelter all the children of one mother and one father. And I saw that it was holy.

—Black Elk Speaks, *The Great Vision*, 1932, p. 36

West Lake Creek is located in the Sawatch Mountain Range, the largest of the ranges in a sub-region of the Rocky Mountains known as the Southern Rockies. It was formed approximately sixty million years ago during a geologic event known as the Laramide Orogeny, a period of mountain building and upheaval responsible for the creation of today's Rocky Mountains. Evidence of this major tectonic process can still be seen, beginning by the Eagle River, just upstream from where the mountains meet the Colorado River, and extending south for almost one hundred miles in a towering wall of peaks that form a distinct north-south boundary and rank as the highest range in the Continental Rocky Mountains.

In geologic time, these sixty million-year-old mountains are relative newcomers. But their entire story spans nearly three billion years, encompassing a complex series of changing environments that reads like a science fiction thriller or primeval mythology. Mountain ranges rise, erode, and are buried in their own debris, only to rise and fall again. Shallow seas sweep across the land, lapping at beaches edged by lush subtropical forests. Volcanoes erupt, searing the earth with lava and filling the air with white-hot ash. While volcanic fires still smolder, rivers of glacial ice tug at summits and scour valleys.

Today, viewed from the high mountain peaks and ridges above and to the south of the property, the wild and varied mountain landscape unfolds like deceptively soft folds of cloth. Lakes, shining like scraps of metal, reflect the sun's rays, while shadows emphasize the undulating nature of the creases of the drainages and valleys below. But it is only from on the ground, when distance is measured in footsteps, that the subtleties of the landscape become apparent. There you feel the steepness of the topography, the rockiness of the ground underneath. There you can see and touch and smell the soil, whose variations of color, texture and moisture convey important information about dry slopes, damp hillsides, and fertile valley loam.

To be in this tranquil setting, tucked in the shadow of New York Mountain and bisected by the meandering turns of West Lake Creek, is to live amid the ancient and hypnotic drama of mountain building, erosion, glacial carving, and the resilience of life in an environment of extremes. It is a place where some of the deepest mysteries of existence are put into perspective.

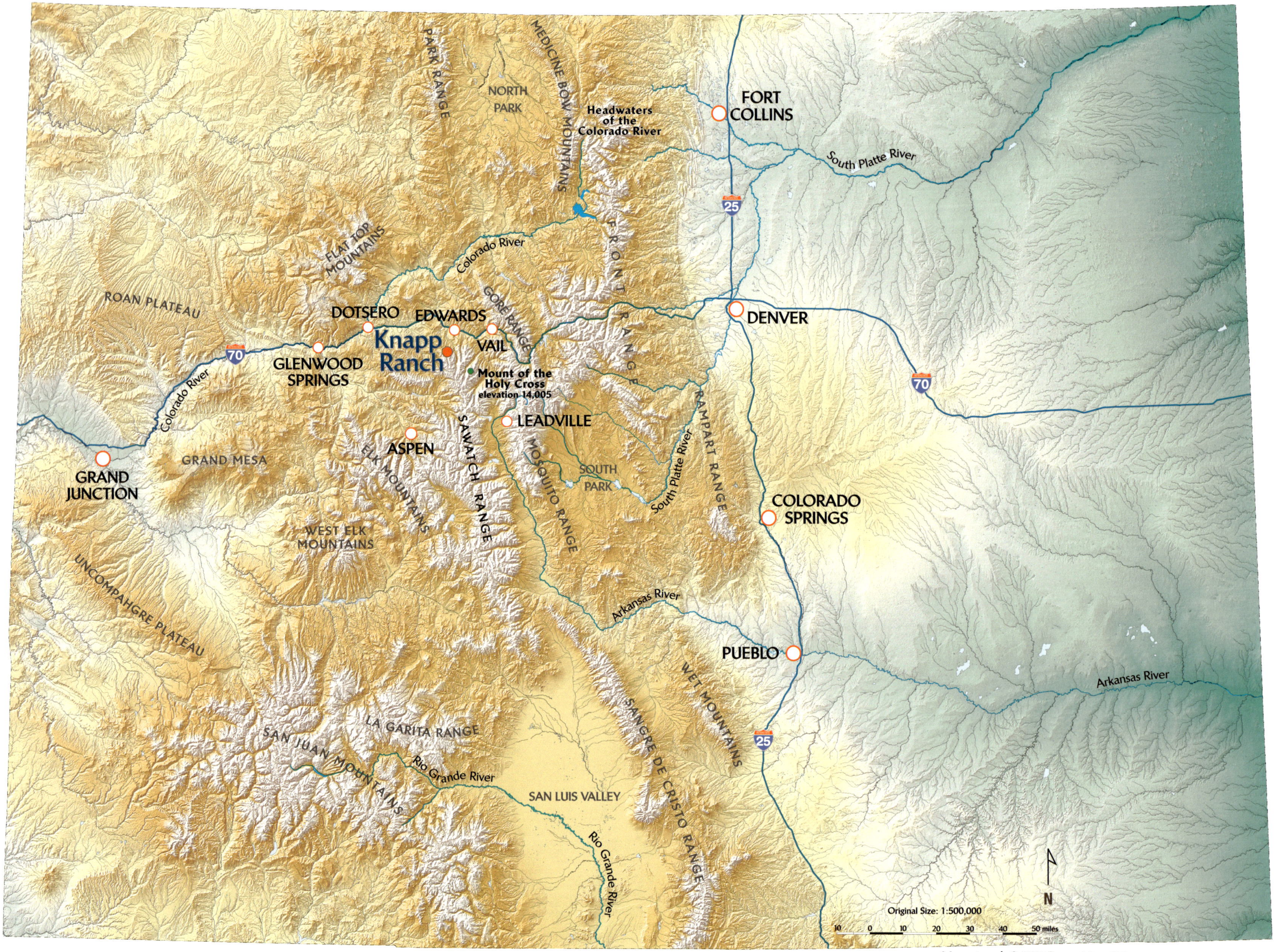

Map artwork © 2000 Raven Maps & Images, www.ravenmaps.com

Knapp Ranch is located in a mountainous region in the northwest quadrant of Colorado. South of the ranch, the Holy Cross Wilderness protects a region of soaring ridges and peaks dotted with alpine lakes, pools, and streams. To the north, dry, south-facing sage-covered slopes rim the Eagle River Valley, which runs east to west from the Continental Divide, past the towns of Avon, Edwards, and Eagle to Dotsero, where it joins the Colorado River.

As the full moon rises on an evening in late June, a cornice of snow clings to the undulating ridgeline along the shoulder of New York Mountain just south of Knapp Ranch. Fading light from the western sky reveals the wavy impressions of "sun cups" in the snow—a phenomenon caused by differential melting of a snowy surface under the intense sunshine found at high altitude.

A large boulder rests on the ridge overlooking the Main Lodge and upper West Lake Creek Valley. Called glacial erratics, these rocks—some comparable in size to small houses—were carried by the glaciers that filled, and ultimately sculpted, the valleys of the Rocky Mountains. After the glaciers receded, the boulders remained and can be seen scattered throughout the woods and meadows at Knapp Ranch. In some cases, cabins and trails have been constructed to incorporate these large and sculptural objects.

Weighing somewhere in the range of thirty tons, the boulder shown in the middle of this photograph came to rest thousands of years ago in a narrow section of West Lake Creek, just below where the cabins at Knapp Ranch are now located. As the boulder continues to weather from erosion caused by snow, ice, and running water, it will eventually break into smaller pieces, until one day it may be reduced to sediment and be washed away entirely.

Weather and its Effect on the Watershed

Natural communities reflect the various living and non-living elements that come together in a place, including plants, animals, soil, water, and climate. The adage, "If you don't like the weather, wait five minutes," accurately reflects the unpredictability and broad scope of climate in the Colorado mountains. Mountain weather conditions are deeply influenced by elevation, with the differences from one area to another clearly imprinted, like a mosaic, on the shape and texture of the landscape. At nine thousand feet above sea level, the effects of wind, water, solar exposure and seasonal change are extreme, and they elicit profound biological responses from the inhabitants of the landscape. The resulting unique behaviors of the animals and plants that survive—and even flourish—in this formidable, elevated region have given rise to a richly diverse native flora and fauna.

These distinct weather conditions are also responsible for the variability of water distribution in the American West. As air rises, it cools, and because cool air cannot retain moisture, storm clouds driven up and over the mountains are forced to release their cargo at higher elevations. As a result of this process, the very water that much of the Western United States relies on for survival is returned to mountainous regions that are simply too cold or too high for significant habitation. That leaves the valleys below—most of which are now densely populated with cities, towns, agriculture and industry—in conflict with one another over water rights and long-term land-and water-use strategies. While elevation may be the primary determining force of natural systems, its ability to influence watersheds is equally important, because it has the power to shape political, demographic, cultural, and geographic boundaries and systems.

Just west of Edwards town center, Lake Creek (a combination of East and West Lake creeks) joins the Eagle River where it heads westward, meeting the Colorado River some twenty-eight miles downstream at Dotsero (aptly named by Ferdinand Hayden as his "Dot Zero" reference point for his 1877 survey maps). The Colorado—a powerful, yet relatively shallow river—is the ninth-longest river in North America, at fourteen hundred fifty miles. Draining almost two hundred fifty thousand square miles in its fourteen-thousand-foot plummet toward the sea, the Colorado is the source for a good portion of the potable and irrigation water for more than thirty million people and more than five million acres of cropland.

At the foot of the flat-topped Gold Dust Peak (13,380 feet), the headwaters of West Lake Creek rest in the tranquility of New York Lake (11,280 feet) before beginning the long journey downstream toward the mighty Colorado River, and, historically, the Gulf of Mexico. The lake, which is not visible from Knapp Ranch, is located approximately six miles to the south and 2,500 feet above the upper West Lake Creek Valley.

In Colorado's Rocky Mountains, tree line occurs between 11,000 and 12,000 feet in elevation. Above that point, trees cannot grow due to frigid soil temperatures and a short growing season. Along the rocky ridgeline near the summit of New York Mountain, shown here, plants of any size are a rare sight, found only in hidden pockets where warmth and moisture collect. In this steep terrain, remnants of windblown cornices of snow cling to the ridge in early June. Most of the snow that falls at these remote heights eventually finds its way to distant reservoirs, farm fields, homes and golf courses by midsummer. In lean years, however, the fragility of high mountain snowpack is further exacerbated by frequent wind and dust storms, and high temperatures.

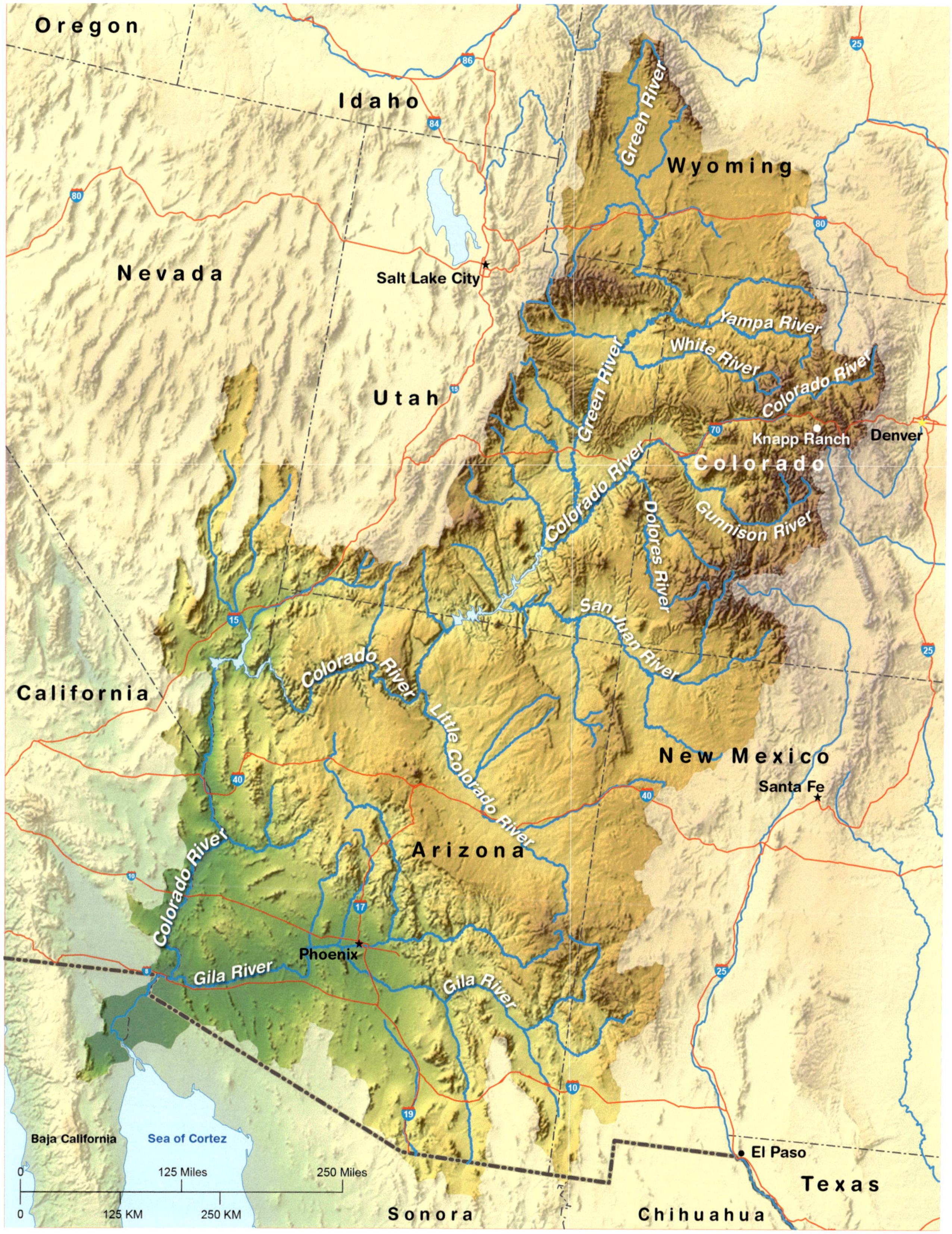

Map artwork © Map Resources

Above: Under the warmth of the intense spring sun, snowpack below New York Mountain melts into the basin and collects in small streams that feed into West Lake Creek. As the creek descends from Knapp Ranch, it increases in size and velocity, joined by other streams on its journey to meet the Eagle River just below the town of Edwards.

Left: The Colorado River is the only generally reliable source of surface water in the American Southwest. Through a series of complex waterworks and diversions developed as a result of the Colorado River Compact of 1922 (a management agreement that apportions water among seven contiguous states), the river provides water to more than thirty million people, most of whom live in the sprawling desert cities of Phoenix, Las Vegas, and Southern California. From its headwaters high in the Colorado Rockies to a now-dry riverbed in Mexico, the river travels over one thousand four hundred and fifty miles, and once reached all the way to the Sea of Cortez. Its water—including the water gathered from the high peaks and ridgelines above Knapp Ranch—is used for irrigation, drinking water, and electricity. What isn't used simply evaporates in the arid Sonoran Desert.

These two photographs, taken from the same location along West Lake Creek below the cabins at Knapp Ranch, illustrate the extreme fluctuations in stream flow throughout the season.

Above: By early June, warm temperatures at higher elevations expedite the melting of the snowpack, creating a deluge of water that frequently overflows the banks of small creeks. In most mountain environments, this annual "peak runoff" flushes creeks and rivers, and recharges the groundwater.

By late October, stream flows are significantly reduced. The low-flow conditions that occur in late autumn and winter can have a serious impact on the health of trout streams. The fish need adequate water depth for cover, protection, and food, and for the cold-water temperatures and increased oxygen that both they and their aquatic invertebrate prey depend on.

The passing of a sudden rainstorm at the end of the valley beyond Knapp Ranch creates a swirling veil of clouds around New York Mountain in early spring.

Changeable Mountain Weather

Claiming approximately 75 percent of the nation's land above 10,000 feet in elevation, including fifty-three peaks of 14,000 feet or higher, and approximately eighteen hundred peaks between 11,000 feet and 14,000 feet in elevation, Colorado is the highest state in the contiguous United States. With an area just over 104,000 square miles, it ranks eighth in size among the fifty states.

With generally higher elevations than the surrounding states, Colorado's climate is relatively cool and dry, and also subject to dramatic and sudden change. In the mountainous areas of central and western Colorado, elevations range from below seven thousand feet in the lower mountain valleys to more than fourteen thousand feet on the highest peaks, resulting in extreme differences in temperature, humidity, precipitation and wind over relatively short distances. Microclimates are common throughout the mountains, offering opportunities for thrifty plants and animals to flourish in protected pockets of warm temperatures and excess moisture.

Summer afternoon temperatures consistently decrease about 4 to 5 degrees Fahrenheit per thousand feet, so while typical July afternoon temperatures in the lower valleys might reach the 70s, 80s, and even 90s, in the higher mountains, temperatures top out in the high 60s and lower 70s. Often, elevation-caused temperature changes are masked by inversions, a condition that occurs frequently in winter when the temperature of the atmosphere increases with altitude. Because cold air is denser than warm air, it tends to collect in mountain valleys and on clear nights, especially during winter when the ground is covered with snow, the coldest temperatures—sometimes as cold as minus 30 degrees Fahrenheit—are found near the center of these high valleys, while higher upslope, the temperatures are considerably warmer.

Wind patterns in the mountains are controlled by topography. Mountain-valley circulations are common, with winds typically blowing up the valley from low to high during the day. At night, those winds reverse to blow down the valleys. Above 11,500 feet, strong winds exceeding between fifty and one hundred miles per hour are common. Extending north and south through the middle of the state, the mountains form a substantial block to regional air motion. As a result, winds in most valleys west of the Continental Divide tend to be less ferocious, especially in fall and winter, while areas along and east of the crest of the Continental Divide are subject to severe, sudden, and devastating downslope windstorms throughout the winter months.

A headwater state, Colorado is a source of four of the nation's major rivers: the Colorado, the Rio Grande, the Arkansas, and the Platte. Precipitation increases with elevation in both winter and summer, but the elevation effect is greatest in midwinter, when winds at the mountaintop level are strongest. Starting in October, high peaks and mountain ranges receive the majority of their precipitation, with snow accumulating in shaded or level areas at elevations above eight thousand feet. Most of the mountains' snowmelt occurs during May and June, with rivers reaching their peak streamflows for the year. Across the globe, however, temperatures are warming due to climate change. Precipitation in March and April arrives in the form of rain, not snow. And the cornices and snowfields found in high mountain cirques melt out much more quickly, leaving the mountains bare of snow by mid-August.

In summer, mountain peaks and ranges are effective thunderstorm generators whenever the regional air masses are sufficiently moist. Most years, local thunderstorms form nearly every afternoon in and near the mountains. The last half of July and much of August are particularly prone to mountain thunderstorms, while June is often a much drier month in the high country. Snow and soft hail are possible from mountain storms any month of the year, even in July and August.

This is a place of incredible adventure and a tiny bit of danger. Lightning strikes on the ridge. Bears nibbling in the bushes. Mountain lions scouting the stream bank. We are more alive here than anywhere else that we have lived. There is a higher power at work here that encourages, even reminds us, to think of our mortality and respect of nature. —Betsy and Bud Knapp

Adapting to the Seasons

Spring is a time of reawakening. Longer days mean short and intense periods of melt-off and spurts of growth, punctuated by heavy, wet snowfall. Temperatures can fluctuate more than 50 degrees in a twelve-hour period. First to melt are the pastures and shrubland hillsides that receive the greatest sun exposure. Even before the snow has fully retreated, the green shoots of early spring plants are pushing through the surly mat of last year's leaf detritus like an eager toddler, determined to make the most of the short growing season ahead.

A rich blanket of green envelops the land in summer, its heavenly veneer revealing the rush of growth occurring beneath its surface. Summer is a time of rapid growth, flowering and setting of seed before the first frosts of autumn, which can often occur in late August. In the aspen groves, a lush understory thrives, including some of the best wildflower displays on the ranch—plants with evocative names such as scarlet paintbrush, Parry's lousewort, mariposa lily, tall chiming bells, orange sneezeweed, coneflower, tall larkspur, monkshood, and blue columbine, the Colorado state flower.

As the days shorten and the sun's arc drops to the south, the cooler temperatures of autumn trigger dramatic change in the resident flora and fauna. The aspen forest transforms from a haven of cool green shade to a cathedral of golden light, and the oak-mountain shrubland comes alive with acorns, fruits and berries, providing a rich smorgasbord for wildlife when conditions are favorable. As fall progresses, the shrubland changes from camouflage green to a display of color resembling a Turkish tapestry, rich with golds, oranges, browns, rusts, and reds.

In winter, only the hardiest creatures can survive the limited food supply and periods of extreme cold. Despite the harsh conditions, many plants and animals have developed diverse and truly intriguing strategies for living in this environment. In the coniferous forests, spruce squirrels feed on cones they buried in the fall, their chatter echoing through the treetops as they warn the forest of predators. Bushy-tailed wood rats, at home in the aspen trees and shrublands, may become unwelcome guests in the cabins or storage buildings, seeking to escape the winter's chill. Moving from willow thicket to forest, snowshoe hares leave their characteristic "big foot" tracks in the fresh powder. Even as the food supply drops, an impressive array of winter resident birds remain—including the downy and hairy woodpecker, Clark's nutcracker, Steller's jay, chickadee, pine grosbeak, Cassin's finch, and pine siskin, as well as several owl species—all surviving the winter months, feeding on seeds of grasses and forbs, oak and conifers, or gleaning dormant insects from in and under tree bark.

Aspen groves typically consist of one or more clonal stands. In autumn, this becomes particularly apparent when the leaves of one clone all change color at the same time, even as a nearby stand remains green a bit longer. Like this stand of aspens growing along the meadow edge in Card Creek west of Knapp Ranch, some trees adopt tinges of red and orange, while others remain vividly golden.

Two photographs of the valley, taken from the ridge above the Main Lodge in early June and in January, reveal the dramatic changes that occur in the mountain landscape in the course of a year. Each season offers its own unique weather, opportunities, and experiences, requiring a certain adaptability and resourcefulness from the valley's residents.

On a dry and sunbaked south-facing slope above the Main Lodge, wild buckwheat sprouts from a small crevice at the edge of an erratic boulder where moisture collects during periodic rains. The solar energy absorbed by the boulder forms a microclimate that propels the growth of surrounding plants, including the colorful patchwork of lichen flourishing on its surface.

Sun-loving aspen stands regenerate through sprouts or suckers produced by their roots in response to increased soil temperatures. As a result, aspens are often the first to colonize forest clearings, burns, or other disturbed sites. However, as stands grow and shade increases, conifers begin to replace the aspen. Here, on a north-facing slope at Knapp Ranch, a small colony of hardy and colorful aspens is interspersed with the snow-dusted monochromatic late autumn conifer landscape.

A healthy aspen grove is dense and opaque. A diseased and dying stand, such as this one located above the cabins at Knapp Ranch, lacks diversity and, in many cases, the aspens are being rapidly replaced by species such as serviceberry, a shrub that is quick to capitalize on sunlight, water, and soil nutrients. The aspen forest is critical to protecting watershed health. Its thick and shallow root system not only holds the soil in place, it also acts as a filtering system, capturing water runoff and cleaning it before it joins a larger aquatic system.

The Adaptable Aspen

One of few deciduous trees found in the Rocky Mountains and the most widespread tree species on the North American continent, aspens are closely associated with seasonal change, particularly in the Central and Southern Rockies. Stately and serene, their white trunks form a transparent screen of playful shadow and light in the dead of winter. In early spring, the trees come alive with soft, furry and pendulous catkins, followed closely by a mist of emerging lime-green leaves. Throughout the summer, the aspen forest provides a canopy of cool, green shelter and filtered shade. Finally, in autumn, it erupts in a fluttering golden tapestry tinged with flecks of orange and crimson.

Aspens reproduce by sending out horizontal root suckers that produce a family that is a genetic clone of the mother tree. That this family is a single organism is quite obvious in the spring, as individual clones tend to leaf out earlier or later than adjacent clones. Similarly, trees that adopt a unique shade of red or orange in fall are typically part of one clone.

Ecologically productive and incredibly resilient, aspen trees function as both protector and provider, buffering the harsh sunlight and dry air, and providing valuable habitat for a wide range of plants, animals and birdlife. Aspens are relatively short-lived; in some instances, they can be a climax forest, but far more commonly their role is as a successional species, naturally designed to serve as a stage in plant cover between disturbances (fires, blowdowns, avalanches, insect outbreaks) and mature conifer-dominated forests.

Like most deciduous trees, aspens expend a lot of energy each spring producing a green transpiring leaf. In fact, one large leafed-out aspen grove can produce enough transpiration to create a microclimate of cooler temperatures and higher humidity significant enough, when combined with a rich understory of herbaceous plants, to act as a natural firebreak. In cases of severe drought, however, an aspen simply is not equipped to pull enough moisture from its roots and trunk into its leaves. This often results in widespread mortality.

In recent years, aspen forests have suffered severe and rapid dieback known as "sudden aspen decline," or SAD. Unlike typical stand-level changes that result from disturbance and succession, SAD is impacting the West's forests on a massive scale. Dendrologists think it is likely that aspen have not reproduced by seed germination since the end of the Pleistocene era, suggesting that they have persisted by virtue of their long-lived root systems instead. It is thought that the overly warm and droughty conditions that existed at the turn of the twenty-first century are to blame for the current onslaught of SAD, with pathogens and insects playing a major role in destroying whole root systems. More often than not, aspen stands with dying trees cannot produce shoots to replace old ones, a situation which in all likelihood is related to years of drought that inflicted deep damage.

Like any forest community, a healthy aspen grove includes sprouts, saplings (middle-aged trees), and mature trees. If no sprouts or saplings are present, the replacement of the grove by grass, shrubs and/or conifers is probably underway.

A handful of Douglas fir trees exist on Knapp Ranch today. Here, a weathered stump is surrounded by a regenerating forest of young aspen trees and shrubs. Located just uphill from the creek bottom, the tree, which likely met its end by fire, wind, or lightning, once cast a dense canopy of shade that stunted surrounding growth. In its absence, sunlight and moisture have hastened the arrival of a new and more diverse forest community.

Above: A common sight on south-facing slopes in spring, multi-flowered phlox grows in and among sagebrush, serviceberry and bitterbrush on the dry slopes above the Main Lodge. Its fragrant nectar attracts butterflies and bees.

Upper right: A gem in the early spring landscape at Knapp Ranch, the mariposa lily has a sweet and edible bulbous root that was often dug and cooked like a potato or ground into flour by Native Americans and early settlers. Pocket gophers and other rodents are attracted to the tasty roots, storing them in caches for winter eating.

Right: Primarily pollinated by queen bees, solitary bees and hummingbirds, the bright blue flowers of Nelson's larkspur dot the south-facing slope above the Main Lodge in June.

The blue columbine is Colorado's state flower, and a lovely reminder of summer in the mountains. Here, a single bloom stands tall among the lupine in the shade of the aspen forest at Knapp Ranch.

Above: The vibrant red foliage of the chokecherry marks the onset of autumn on a south-facing slope above the Main Lodge on Knapp Ranch.

Left: Known for its profusion of white flowers in spring and dark blue berries in fall, serviceberry is a staple shrub on the south-facing slopes above the Main Lodge, providing food and shelter for wildlife and birds. Although bears prefer chokecherries and acorns, serviceberries are equally important to their high-fat, pre-hibernation diet. Native Americans used the fruit to help make a nutritious high-protein food called pemmican, a concentrated mixture of dried ground meat, melted animal fat, and dried berries. They also found serviceberry's hard, straight-grained wood ideal for making arrow shafts, spears, and digging tools.

Often seen on open slopes and wooded areas throughout Knapp Ranch, wild roses bloom in June, producing hundreds of fragrant, saucer-shaped pink flowers that are attractive to bees and other pollinators. High in vitamins C and A, the fruit of the flower, called the rose hip, can be dried and powdered for soups, boiled for jellies, or consumed as an energy food. Native Americans used the entire shrub, making tea from its leaves to treat stomach ailments, and boiling the buds, petals, stems, and root bark into a tea for eye problems—particularly snow blindness. Rose buds and blossoms are traditional ingredients in moisturizing cosmetics.

Western red columbine, a local favorite for its vibrant orange and red blooms, grows on the moist and shady hillsides at Knapp Ranch. Native Americans used the plant medicinally, massaging the columbine's ripe seeds into their hair to discourage lice. The seeds are no longer recommended for medicinal use, as they are toxic when consumed in large amounts.

In the forest at Knapp Ranch, aspens display the claw marks, or "arborglyphs," of black bears. Bears typically climb trees to avoid conflict with humans, dogs, or other bruins, and they forage on the trees' spring buds and snack on any birds' eggs they might find. A familiar sight in aspen forests and oak-mountain shrublands where berries proliferate, bears eat grass, forbs, fruit, acorns, insects, and honey, including the comb and the bees.

A fox, its legs wet from hunting in deep wet grass, balances on top of a rail fence on a neighboring property. Though celebrated in literature and legend for its secretive, sly nature, the fox is one of the most visible wild residents, and can become habituated to human presence very easily.

Who Else Lives Here?

Protected by surrounding mountains and forests at nine thousand feet, Knapp Ranch is located at the upper limit of the hospitable montane life zone, a vegetative zone defined by aspen forest, as well as riparian and coniferous ecosystems, the biological and physical communities that are most representative of the Southern Rockies. The more extreme subalpine and alpine life zones are visible to the south of the property, extending upwards to the indomitable ridge of mountains above.

The differing environments found throughout the ranch nurture an abundance of wildlife. Emerging from hibernation in mid-March, bears feed on tender buds and aspen catkins in spring, transitioning to carbohydrate-rich roots, berries and acorns in September. Elk browse, graze, and seek cover in the shadows of the forest as the herds migrate from winter to summer range and back again. Mule deer pass through the aspen groves, nibbling on new growth and bedding down in the soft underbrush. Evidence of porcupines, squirrels, deer mice, voles, and weasels are found in the midden (a term whose literal translation is "garbage dump") at the base of trees, and in the gnaw, the claw marks visible on tree bark.

The mountain meadows that form the valley floor are a haven for certain predators—coyote, fox, badger, weasel and hawks—in search of rodents that burrow in the protective shelter of the tall grass. From the cirques and lakes high above, the waters of West Lake Creek flow through the heart of the ranch, providing the lifeblood of the property, rich in the necessary comforts of food and shelter. In the creek bottom, plants and animals congregate, finding refuge and places to drink, nest or rest in the tall willows and thick vegetation.

Poets and naturalists, and indeed storytellers of all kinds, have remarked on the importance of nature in our lives, reminding us that we are but tiny specks in the great continuum of time. The reverence and respect given to Mother Earth by Native Americans point to a deeper, more spiritual connection that comes from a reciprocal relationship between the land and the people who inhabit it. Acknowledging and honoring the beauty and majesty of our surroundings is but a small way to show our gratitude for the opportunity to inhabit this place.

You don't have to be native to a place to maintain a spiritual relationship with it, of course. Rather, that relationship comes from living in and with nature, an experience that puts our existence in context with something much older and certainly more powerful, than ourselves. David Brower, founder of Friends of the Earth and the first Executive Director of the Sierra Club, suggested that the wild world fills man's need for an environment "where he can be reminded that civilization is only a thin veneer over the deep evolutionary flow of things that built him." Edward Abbey, an outspoken defender of the wilderness, wrote that immersing oneself in the wild country has the power to remind civilized people to be humble in the face of it, for "out there is a different world, older and greater and deeper by far than ours, a world which surrounds and sustains the little world of men as sea and sky surround and sustain a ship." That momentous strength we gain from being in wild places is supplemented by the gifts of curiosity, empathy, and ritual that come from watching the clouds billow over the mountain peaks, smelling the earthy goodness of the sage and wild grass after a summer rain shower, dipping our toes in crystal-clear water, or watching a herd of elk graze quietly in the meadow at sundown. These are the gifts we receive when we acknowledge the land that nurtures us all.

A shy and elusive mountain lion is caught by a camera trap in the forested area along West lake Creek. With a home range of between fifteen and over three hundred square miles, adult lions can travel twenty or more miles a day in search of food. Just as deer and elk populations are increasing in the lower valleys, so too are mountain lion sightings, a sign that the big cats are following their prey closer to areas of human habitation.

Bucks in full velvet, startled by a sudden noise, freeze in place on the dry slopes overlooking the Main Lodge. Mule deer browse on native shrubs, grasses, and forbs, migrating in winter to south-facing slopes, where the snowpack is shallower or absent due to sun exposure, and the sage is plentiful.

There is an animal inside with the smell of us fresh in its nostrils. I realize that it had not been attacking us. We would have been easy to catch. Instead, the sound of its voice was strictly territorial, designed to root down into our spines and trigger a flight response. We did as we were told. We answered the animal clearly, playing our part in the conversation with everything we had. —Craig Childs, *The Animal Dialogues*

A bull elk passes under a canopy of branches in early autumn. The bull's antlers, its most eye-catching feature, are made of bone and can weigh up to thirty pounds. By late winter, the elk sheds its antlers, and within two weeks, new growth begins.

Two cow elk and their calves pause on a rocky knoll overlooking the meadow at Knapp Ranch in midsummer. During autumn, larger herds gather at dusk in the meadows throughout upper West Lake Creek for the annual rut, or mating ritual. A staple of Native American and Anglo hunters for centuries, elk declined so dramatically during the late 1800s that Colorado had to initiate a statewide hunting ban and supplement its own population through the reintroduction of a few hundred elk, which were shipped by train from Yellowstone National Park.

Above: Frequently glimpsed along West Lake Creek and neighboring Card Creek, beavers are vegetarians, subsisting entirely on the leaves, stems, and bark of willow, aspen, and cottonwood. Beavers gnaw off branches and fell entire trees to construct their lodges and dams, causing tremendous wear and tear on their teeth. To keep pace with the incessant grinding, a beaver's teeth simply never stop growing. The combination of a harder outer layer of enamel and a slightly softer inner layer of dentin makes for a self-sharpening system that's at work with every bite.

Right: In nearby Card Creek, a beaver's lodge, dome-shaped and thatched with branches and mud, is located in the middle of a wetland habitat most likely created by the animal's savvy engineering talent. The wet meadows and wetlands that result from beaver dams support a diversity of keystone species and abundant populations of plants, animals, birds, insects, and fish. Beaver ponds function as a sink for carbon, nitrogen and other nutrients, effectively removing pollutants from the water before it continues downstream.

Until the late 1970s, moose were a rare sight in Colorado. Today, the population is thriving, thanks to a successful reintroduction effort by Colorado Parks and Wildlife. Most moose are found in mountain wetland and riparian habitat, where they browse on willows, their primary food source. Moose have been seen swimming across the lake, walking casually along the roads at Knapp Ranch, and browsing the willows along the creek—a sure sign that they are migrating through the upper West Lake Creek Valley.

A common sight during midwinter at Knapp Ranch, a red fox quietly rests at the edge of the forest, listening for the sound of voles and deer mice moving under the snow. Its acute hearing allows it to locate small mammals in the subnivean zone, the space where the surface of the ground and the bottom of the snowpack meet.

Now and then we hear the wilder voices of the wilderness, from animals that in the hours of darkness do not fear the neighborhood of man: the coyotes wail like dismal ventriloquists, or the silence may be broken by the snorting and stamping of a deer. — Teddy Roosevelt

A coyote, captured at dusk, pads softly across the snow in search of squirrels, voles, mice and other small rodents. At night, coyote yips can often be heard echoing across the valley.

Left: A male dusky grouse struts along an aspen rail on a neighboring property. In full courtship display, males fan their tails, hop, strut, and hoot—fluttering their wings so loudly they can often be heard half a mile away.

© Greg Lasley/VIREO

Far left: A mountain chickadee, identifiable by its signature white eyebrow, clings to a snowy branch. When spruce and lodgepole cones open in September, these birds are known to work from dawn to dusk, gathering and storing seeds for winter.

Left: An American dipper prepares to dive off a rock in West Lake Creek just below the cabins. The most aquatic of all songbirds, the dipper is adept at swimming underwater to capture food in cold and clear mountain streams. Key indicators of stream quality, dippers feed on mayfly and caddisfly larvae, which are typically present only in clean, well-aerated water.

Upper left: Mountain bluebirds can be seen flitting about in the meadows and along the forest edges at Knapp Ranch, their brilliant blue hue a welcome sign of springtime in the mountains. Nest boxes attached to fence posts provide opportunities for bluebirds to nest when natural cavities are not available.

Above: The white-crowned sparrow lives in the shrubby understory of alpine riparian thickets and boggy willow woodlands, feeding on beetles, spiders, and caterpillars. In early spring, the birds are commonly seen in the willows along West Lake Creek, feasting on catkins.

Left: With strikingly beautiful plumage that resembles silk, a pair of cedar waxwings gather sage and other material from the dry slopes above the Main Lodge for a nest. Waxwings nest in midsummer, later than most other songbirds, because they need ripe berries (serviceberry and currant) to feed their young.

© Glenn Bartley

Above: A common sight at birdfeeders around Knapp Ranch, the Steller's jay is known for its flash of vibrant blue and loud raspy call. These birds are often found mimicking other birds, particularly red-tailed hawks, as well as squeaky doors and telephones.

Upper right: The Clark's nutcracker, frequently observed perching at the very top of conifer trees around Knapp Ranch, is well known for its nasal and raucous call. Possessing its own version of an internal GPS, the nutcracker is capable of burying up to thirty-three thousand food items in thousands of locations on south-facing slopes, and then finding them months later by utilizing spatial references to surrounding objects, such as stumps, trees, and boulders.

Right: Often found in dense swarms around birdfeeders at the ranch, the black rosy-finch rarely descends below seven thousand feet, preferring to forage in areas on and around alpine snowfields.

The smallest woodpecker in North America, the downy woodpecker marks its territory by drumming on trees. At Knapp Ranch, it can be found foraging for wood-boring insects on tree trunks in the aspen forest.

A male evening grosbeak rests on an aspen branch. Grosbeaks dominate ranch birdfeeders in winter, pushing other birds out of the way and creating a cacophony of noise and flurry. During breeding season, however, the birds are quiet and secretive. Evening grosbeaks feed heavily on spruce budworm, thereby helping to keep this potentially devastating forest pest in check.

Often seen riding the thermals overhead in search of food, the red-tailed hawk uses its extraordinary eyesight to hunt for mice and other rodents in the lower meadows at Knapp Ranch. Recognized by their signature "red tail" and shrill cry, the hawks prefer to live in a semi-open habitat, nesting in aspens and spruce, and on any high perch or rocky outcrop.

© Glenn Bartley

Above: Known for their large "ear" tufts, great horned owls reside in the dense conifer forests at Knapp Ranch, often appropriating the old nests of other larger raptors and squirrels. Nocturnal hunters, owls swoop in on mice, voles, and other rodents.

Left: The once-endangered bald eagle is now a fairly common sight in the lower reaches of Colorado's mountain valleys. In the West Lake Creek Valley, lone bald and golden eagles have been observed perched high in the treetops.

To have passed through life and never experienced solitude is to have never known oneself. To have never known oneself is to have never known anyone.

— Joseph Wood Krutch

Articulating our conceptual ideas was the easy part; learning how to live in a rural mountain valley was more difficult. Our role was to imbue this place with heart and soul, and to reinforce the concepts of quality, simplicity, and responsible use. We let the land, its history, and the experts advise us on how best to accomplish this. —Betsy and Bud Knapp

2

DISCOVERY

IMAGINATION BECOMES REALITY

Settling Lake Creek

The history of Lake Creek abounds with stories of hardy folks settling and finding community in this remote and rocky environment. Written accounts, though plentiful, really only begin after the arrival of Euro-American settlers. Evidence uncovered by archaeologists at sites along the Colorado River suggests that prehistoric people inhabited the Eagle River Valley year-round, traveling up East and West Lake creeks to hunt and gather in the summer months. Locally, the Ute Indians—Colorado's longest continuous inhabitants—hunted, fished, and foraged for food in the Lake Creek Valley.

One of the area's first hunting and fishing lodges was located on a bluff overlooking the confluence of Lake Creek and the Eagle River. Established in 1879 by Joseph Brett, an entrepreneurial florist from the French province of Alsace-Lorraine, the place—known as "The Frenchman's"—consisted mainly of tents (for sleeping, gaming and drinking), and an area for shooting. Rules for guests included "no rowdiness, no hot water, wash up at the trough." Inquisitive and socially adept, Brett was a stalwart of the local community and quick to lend a hand when needed. He led hunting and fishing expeditions throughout the area, providing his family and guests with smoked venison and fresh trout. His vegetable and flower gardens were known far and wide for their bountiful harvest, which sustained his family and others through the seasons. He even befriended a local band of Ute Indians, regularly inviting them into the ranch compound for a hot meal. In return for his hospitality, the Utes performed ceremonial dances in the front yard.

Farther up the creek on the site of the current Knapp Ranch, a lone bachelor named Joseph Vilda homesteaded on one hundred sixty acres. Born in Wilbur, Nebraska, in 1867, Vilda was one of ten boys born to Czech settlers who arrived in Nebraska by way of New Orleans and the Mississippi River. Joe and his brother Fred were the first family members to venture west to Colorado. Settling in upper West Lake Creek in 1901, Joe Vilda trapped bear, grazed animals, and grew lettuce on his property. Old-timers recall his porch strewn with animal hides, drying in the sun.

Forced, for unknown reasons, to mortgage his homestead in 1923, Vilda transferred the property to Thomas J. Dice, a realtor and former Eagle County commissioner. There is no recorded history of the land for the next decade, but it is believed that Vilda continued to rent the property from Dice until 1938, when he moved to a small cabin on lower Lake Creek. He died in 1948 at the age of eighty-one in Eagle.

In 1942, Dice's wife sold the land to adjoining landowner and sawmill operator JD Riggs for $1,800. In addition to growing crops and raising cattle, Riggs hauled lumber for the mines located in the mountains above the property. Like Vilda, Riggs had the reputation of killing more bears than any other man in Eagle County. According to some of the historic anecdotes in the Eagle County archives, he could be somewhat overzealous in his desire to own land, and he had been known to adjust his property corners on occasion in order to get more acreage.

Local rancher Roger Pilgrim and his wife purchased the Riggs Ranch, grazing sheep on the seven-hundred-acre property from 1957 until 1970, when they sold it to a group of Denver-based investors called the New York Mountain Group. Hoping to strike it rich in the building boom leading up to the proposed 1976 Olympic Games, this group put forward a plan to develop one hundred eighty-five homesites in a community called Tenderwild in the West Lake Creek Valley.

When Colorado voters turned down the opportunity to host the Olympics, however, all land development proposals in the West Lake Creek Valley stopped in their tracks, and once again the area became a destination for adventurous locals—including Vail realtor George Lamb. An avid hiker, cross-country skier and open-space advocate, Lamb made it a priority to quietly keep an eye out for an individual or couple with a conservation ethic who would appreciate and preserve the valley's unspoiled beauty. Curious about the web of road infrastructure that was in place in the otherwise empty valley, Lamb spent endless hours researching the property, uncovering ownership information that reached back to the turn of the century, and identifying multiple encumbrances, including the plan for Tenderwild. "I became very possessive of the land after that," Lamb says, devoting much of his spare time to quietly tracking down the ownership group. Serendipitously, Lamb and Bud and Betsy Knapp became acquainted in 1987, during golf lessons. "At the end of our three days together, the Knapps threw me a softball. Did I know of any special pieces of land in the West, and better yet, did I know of anything in the Vail Valley?" Galvanized by the thought that the Knapps' vision for the area might align with his own, Lamb shared his knowledge of the upper West Lake Creek Valley, while acknowledging the complications inherent in the ownership entities. His real estate tenacity paid off: "I knew immediately that whatever the Knapps chose to do here would be of the highest quality and, more importantly, it would integrate with the surrounding environment," Lamb says today.

Courtesy of Eagle County Historical Society, Eagle Valley Library District

Ferdinand Hayden was one of four expedition leaders assigned to survey the Rocky Mountains for the United States government, exploring the region and documenting its features. In 1873, Hayden ventured into the mountains of the Colorado Territory, determined to find the location of the Mount of the Holy Cross. The expedition's maps, photographs, drawings, and newspaper reports helped to demystify the region for a generation of Americans. As a result, fortune hunters, land seekers, and tourists poured into the state. Some sought gold, some homesteaded, some merely admired the scenery and returned home to tell their friends about it. Hayden Geological Survey photographer William Henry Jackson captured this view of the Lake Creek Valley and New York Mountain sometime between 1886 and 1890 from a natural bench above the confluence of Lake Creek and the Eagle River.

Courtesy of the Don Simonton Collection

Courtesy of the Don Simonton Collection

Courtesy of the Don Simonton Collection

Courtesy of the Don Simonton Collection

Above: A photograph depicts the view looking northeast over the Brett Ranch toward the Eagle River in the early 1900s. Today, Interstate 70 parallels the river on the far side, and the community of Edwards extends to the east and northeast of the Brett homestead, shown in the upper right-hand section of the photograph.

Right: One of the area's first hunting and fishing lodges, "The Frenchman's" was located at the confluence of Lake Creek and the Eagle River. Its proprietor, Joseph Brett, led hunting and fishing expeditions throughout the area. In the top photo, Brett (third from right) poses with a group of fishermen from Leadville, c. 1898. Brett also fashioned an area for his guests to shoot skeet within his compound, c. 1895, and offered horseback rides for children.

Courtesy of Eagle County Historical Society, Eagle Valley Library District

In 1901, Joseph Vilda homesteaded on one hundred and sixty acres in the upper West Lake Creek Valley on the site of the modern-day Knapp Ranch. Born in Wilbur, Nebraska, in 1867, Vilda was one of ten sons of a Czech couple who came to Nebraska by way of New Orleans and the Mississippi River. Joe and his brother Fred were the first family members to venture west to Colorado. He trapped bear, raised livestock, and grew lettuce on his property. Old-timers recall seeing his porch strewn with animal hides, drying in the sun. A few remnants of his cabin, located at the south end of the property, still remain, as shown on page 82. Here, Vilda sits on a sawhorse in front of the cabin near Edwards that he moved to later in life, c. early 1900s.

Knapp Ranch Archives

A visitor surveys the upper West Lake Creek Valley, c. 1970s. It was from this very point that Bud and Betsy Knapp first looked out over the open landscape to the peaks in the distance. The seasonal pond is visible in the lower left corner of the photo.

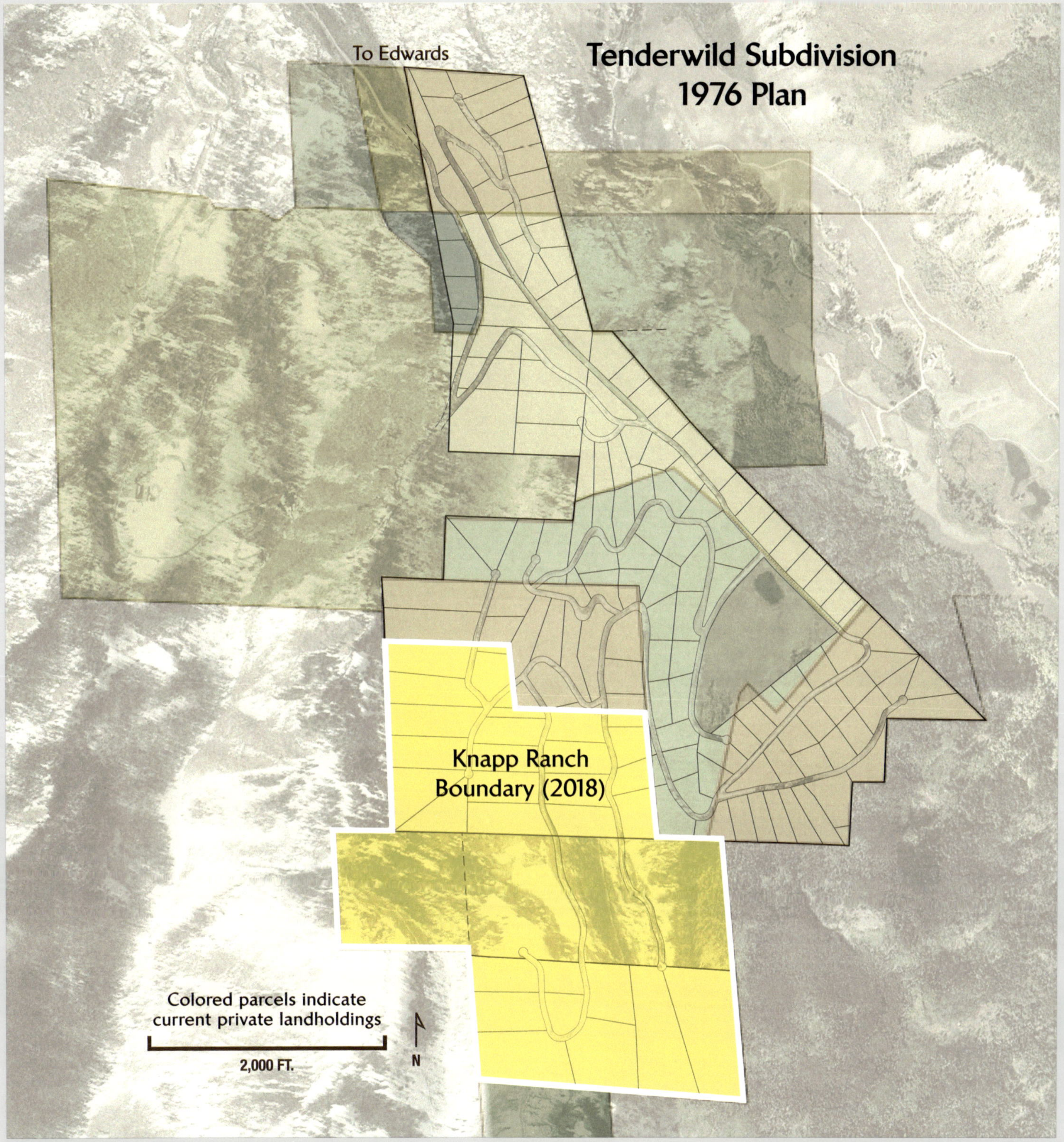

Map by Carly Klein

The proposed Tenderwild subdivision would have stretched the length of the West Lake Creek Valley if built, covering much of the open meadows and wooded areas, up to and including Knapp Ranch (outlined in white on the map).

Tenderwild: The Rise and Fall of an Olympic Village

In 1970, the International Olympic Committee named Denver the host city for the 1976 Games. Some of the alpine events were possibly going to be held at Vail or nearby at Beaver Creek, a resort that had yet to be built. Rampant land speculation followed, fueling a battle between longtime ranchers and environmentalists, and landowners and newcomers eager to make a quick buck. In the crosshairs was a seven-hundred-acre parcel of land in the upper West Lake Creek Valley that had been owned by local rancher Roger Pilgrim since 1957.

In July 1971, the *Eagle Valley Enterprise* reported that "land development throughout the county continues on the upward swing and it appears that anyone who owns land in the county is sitting on a gold mine. …"[1] Sensing opportunity, Pilgrim sold his property to a group of investors, and moved to Wyoming.

Hoping to strike it rich in an Olympics-inspired building boom, this enterprising group went ahead with every intention of developing the property into a dense community of homes, which they called Tenderwild.

At the same time, however, environmentalists, led by state representatives Richard Lamm and Bob Jackson, were at the forefront of widespread opposition to the Olympic bid. In November of 1972, voters in a state considered by many to be the nation's ski capital turned down the opportunity to host the Olympics. The costs, they said, were simply too high. As one newspaper editorial put it, "Ten days of the Olympics will spotlight and attract growth to Denver, Vail and Steamboat Springs, which no longer need it", and, as a consequence, the environment would be ruined forever.[2]

The Tenderwild developers retreated, leaving behind abandoned roads and stacks of unpaid property taxes. A few years later, another group of investors purchased land at the head of the valley, adjacent to what is now Knapp Ranch. Their short-lived proposal ultimately faded as well. And once again the vacant valley was returned to adventurous locals who embraced the opportunity to hike, ski, and picnic in this spectacular setting.

[1] "Booming Land Development," *Eagle Valley Enterprise*, July 8, 1971, no. 38, vol. 72.
[2] Lell, Kathy. "Olympics Again," *Eagle Valley Enterprise*, November 2, 1972.

Discovering the Dream

In 1990, the upper West Lake Creek Valley was picturesque, rugged, and uninhabited. From the top of the hill on the northern boundary, the land dropped away in distinct sections. Directional changes revealed new vistas and changes in vegetation patterns. Along the western edge of the property, views to the north offered glimpses of the Gore Range in the distance. Just under the ridge lay an amphitheater-shaped meadow, dotted with boulders and sagebrush. In the center of this naturally carved glacial bowl, a seasonal wetland—also known as a vernal pool—appeared every year, collecting runoff, wildflowers, frogs, and salamanders in the spring, only to evaporate into a cracked and barren surface of hard clay come midsummer. Farther to the east and hidden in the dense aspen forest, the overgrown Hawley-Reese irrigation ditch carried water from a point upstream to surrounding properties. Flanked by heavily treed slopes to either side, the valley's bottom was alive with the sounds of water and birds. Stately evergreens announced the presence of the creek as it meandered through a warren of beaver ponds, disappearing into dense and overgrown willow stands. At the valley's south end, snow-capped peaks stood sentinel over the land, claiming their stake in the eternal march of history.

For many years, Betsy and Bud had dreamed of finding a place in the country where they could build a home and grow their own food. The chance to fulfill their longtime dream to re-create some of their favorite childhood experiences—Betsy had roamed the woods and lakes of northern Wisconsin, and Bud has always loved the desert Southwest—was exciting. Bud attributes his love of the wide-open spaces of Colorado and Arizona to two men: his grandfather, Cleon T. Knapp, and the American writer and naturalist, Joseph Wood Krutch. An influential statesman in Arizona, Cleon Knapp was an attorney for Phelps Dodge Corporation who helped Arizona gain statehood in the early part of the twentieth century. He was also deeply involved in the development of the Colorado River Compact of 1922. "He had a great pride of place," says Bud Knapp. "I got a bellyful of history, geology, and appreciation for water and the open landscape around me from him, and I became enamored. Even though I wasn't old enough to understand it, I knew it was good and it was beautiful. And that's why, from Los Angeles, I looked out as far as I could for something to replicate that experience." Joseph Wood Krutch's *Desert Year*, published in 1952, also had a profound influence on Bud. Writing evocatively about the natural world, describing the life forms that somehow prosper despite the harsh desert environment, Krutch highlighted the courage and ingenuity needed to make the best of the world as you find it.

The solitude of this place appealed to me a great deal. The simplicity of life and the values held by the people in the rural territory of Colorado were refreshing. You can accomplish a heck of a lot here with a simple handshake. That means a lot to me at this point in my life. —Bud Knapp

High-altitude altocumulus clouds, their swirling bands uplit by the reflective orange and red hues of a setting sun, foretell a change in the weather.

The sharp light that follows an afternoon rain shower reveals a fresh landscape of green, yellow, and red, the distinctive colors of late August in the mountains. This was the view of the valley that first captured the Knapps' imagination.

ESSAY

Designing for Place: Using the Land as a Guide

Rick Lamb, Landscape Architect, ASLA
Cambridge, Massachusetts

Courtesy of Rick Lamb

Midway through design of the Prudential Center's new garden in Boston in 1990, my brother, George Lamb, telephoned to ask if we would be interested in joining a team that was designing a family compound west of Vail. I jumped on the plane and winged my way to Colorado.

As we tromped through the snow during my first visit to the property, my brother pointed out interesting landmarks. Focusing our attention on a horizontal line running the distance of the eastern flank of the property, he described how, in the early years of the twentieth century, the railroad had constructed a wooden sluiceway to bring water from the upper reaches of West Lake Creek to a seasonal wetland where lettuce was grown, and shipped to points east and west. The scars left by a series of road cuts through the valley floor were more recent, made in anticipation of the 1976 Olympic Games by a development group that had high hopes of creating a luxury bedroom community. Down by the creek, the remnants of an old cabin reminded us that hardy souls had inhabited this valley long before we got here.

Our role on this project was to analyze the property, and find the best possible locations for multiple building sites based on views, topography, exposure, vegetation, taking into account any additional contributing environmental and permitting factors. Even though I had been to Colorado numerous times, my knowledge of Western land-use law and planning protocol was fairly limited. For example, I was taken aback by the intricacies of securing water to create and sustain a proposed lake. As a professor of landscape architecture, I had encouraged my students to think about water in the landscape. But it had never occurred to me that any planning and design would be contingent on a complex permit that we would have to obtain from the U.S. Army Corps of Engineers in order to actually use the water that flowed so freely through the property. In addition, because the majority of my work at the time was for resort developers, my immediate tendency was to see valleys as optimal sites for golf courses, with condominiums lining the sides of the adjacent hills. During our first visit together, property owner Bud Knapp set me straight as he said, quite bluntly, "The valley is very special to us, so put aside your resort thinking, and let's consider how we're really going to live here."

At the time I was working on this project, I was on the faculty at Harvard, and working with Bud was almost like working with a senior student. I wouldn't give a lecture, but I would share a vision of what I was looking at: What caught my eye, what was important, and what wasn't. After I had shared my thoughts on a subject, Bud would politely point out the implications of my proposal. He was exceedingly well educated in terms of design and the politics of people. It was a very fun project from our standpoint because we don't normally have clients who are so interested and involved, and who have so much to contribute.

What continues to amaze me is how Betsy Knapp was able to put together a story about the architecture that spoke to the hearts of the people that built the architecture. She was able to create an environment that looked as if it had always been there, including the way things worked, the furniture, and details. Every formula that we learned in school was included in the story. The incredible resource of time is needed to successfully complete a project like this, and do the research on the furniture, along with the details. Experiencing the Knapp Ranch isn't like going to the fanciest antique dealer, or to a resort where everything is perfect and all-inclusive: If you're a guest there, you are invited—even encouraged—to participate in it to the fullest extent possible. ◻

Assembling a Team

Soon after the Knapps took possession of the property, they began to learn about the land in a thorough and strategic way. Carefully articulating the ideas they wanted the property to embody, they let realtor George Lamb assemble a team of experts to develop an appropriate plan. The key to success, they felt, was an approach that stressed humility, patience, and a willingness to seek advice for answers to questions they did not know. Guiding their vision was a reverence for the natural and cultural history of the land on which they were building. Who better to lead that process than their friend George Lamb, a longtime local and authority on design and building in the Vail Valley? "George showed us the property, organized and executed the purchase, and guided the conversations about how to use the land with an artistry and creativity that fit so beautifully with Betsy and me," recalls Bud Knapp, with a fondness that remains unchanged more than twenty-five years later. Their friend Jim McHugh, a photographer with a keen interest in architecture and preservation, describes the process as one of immediate connection with the place and the people. "Because of their interest in design and history—be it antiques or buildings—the Knapps have a real desire to keep that valley as it is. As time goes by, this notion will become increasingly valuable almost everywhere. There's a real sense of past and future happening at the same time there. They have an eye to the future, but they also understand the tradition from which the place comes."

Typically, one of the first consultants to join a project is an architect, engaged by the owner to articulate a vision for how to inhabit a place. The Knapps' strong desire to be responsible stewards, however, required that they first find someone who knew the area well and could assist them in assembling a team of professionals—experts in areas such as climatology, water rights, archaeology, forestry, and land use—someone who recognized the inherent environmental value of the property to the community, and to the region. George Shaeffer, a general contractor who had developed a reputation for quality work and business acumen, turned out to be just the right fit. A fourth-generation Coloradan, Shaeffer knew the region like the back of his hand. If he hadn't seen it from horseback, he'd skied across it. His role from the beginning was to lead the project, provide advice, and oversee the land-improvement efforts. Ultimately, Shaeffer was responsible for assembling the design team and finding the best craftsmen to complete the job. "We were lucky to find people who thought about the land first," Bud Knapp recalls. "Vistas and open space were more important than a building to them."

Many people move into a new home without first experiencing the natural environment in which that home is located—a decision that can alter the way in which a homeowner ultimately inhabits a place. "We had to experience it for ourselves," says Betsy Knapp. "There were so many things we wouldn't know unless we spent time studying it." Ultimately, the Knapps rented an RV, affectionately dubbed the "Minnie Winnie," and spent time getting to know their new property. "It was a valuable experience because it really made us think about what it was we were trying to achieve by living in a place like this," says Betsy. At the time, both of them were busy directing their respective companies and building a second home in Bel Air, California. Time to be alone was precious; time away from meetings, decisions, and other commitments was almost unheard of. "What would it be like for us to settle into a place of such incredible beauty and simply unplug? What would happen when we reached that moment of Nirvana where the left side of our brains—the one that programs us to be busy all the time—simply disengaged?" Could the two of them, Betsy wondered, learn to enjoy this place for what it is and reunite with their spiritual selves?

Betsy Knapp

The Knapps' first official home on the property was a Minnie Winnie.

A century after Joseph Vilda settled along West Lake Creek, the remnants of his cabin are slowly being reclaimed by nature.

Learning From Experts: Land Ownership and Water Rights

George Shaeffer set in motion a property analysis process led by Massachusetts-based landscape architect Rick Lamb (George Lamb's brother), and attorney Greg Kerwin of the Denver-based law firm Gibson Dunn—experts in land planning and Western water issues, respectively. Kerwin, a litigation lawyer, facilitated the privatization of several county roads that had been established during the course of the proposed Tenderwild development process, untangling a complicated web of land ownership and access issues in the valley that dated back to the original homesteaders. A Colorado native and an avid history buff, Kerwin fondly recalls his early work on the property: "Reviewing the homestead files for this property was fascinating. For a valley with a unique and varied history, this was a very inaccessible place. The papers from the Knapps' property indicate that there was quite a bit of friction here amongst the various settlers. Perhaps one person was trying to claim-jump the other in order to obtain their homestead right. Ironically, nothing has changed today."

Rick Lamb spent months scouting the property for the best building sites, and clarifying potentially complicated political and legal issues that might arise with the neighboring parcels, including access and the privatization and vacation, or complete abandonment, of existing easements. For Lamb, understanding the land and the impacts of living in a high-altitude environment were fundamental to the process. "The first thing we did," he says, "was study the land in all seasons. For two years, we saw it in the spring; we watched the colors change in fall, and we trudged on snowshoes through the snow in the middle of January."

As Lamb quickly discovered, elevation is a formidable constraint in the mountain landscape. Even in a protected valley such as upper West Lake Creek, higher elevation means longer-lasting snow cover, stronger winds, colder and thinner soils, and more intense ultraviolet rays. At high altitudes, the incidence of year-round frost is higher, and the range of temperature fluctuation in a 24-hour period is greater. The ground freezes deeper and stays frozen longer. Mountain topography—gentle or rugged—can pose design challenges that easily deter the timid. Conversely, it can also offer the opportunity to create something entirely unique to the physical setting and landscape character. Such was the case with the vernal pool. Re-establishing this existing feature, and developing a larger body of water adjacent to it in the natural bowl, seemed an obvious next step, Lamb says, particularly because the Knapps had a keen desire to maintain and enhance the existing water resources. They envisioned the kind of delightful lake environment that would attract a myriad of wildlife and birds, and also be useful to the owners, providing opportunities for fishing and boating along with fire mitigation and water storage.

A New England native, Lamb is quick to admit his naiveté on the complex subject of Western water rights. "The most important thing I learned on this project is that water rights are fundamentally a very big deal in this part of the country. It never occurred to me that a property owner would have to get a permit to use the water that runs through his property." Deciphering Colorado water law, however, was a task as Sisyphean as making water run uphill, and the process itself took over two years to complete. "In order to develop the ponds," explains Kerwin, "we had to have them decreed as water rights in the water court, not a difficult item to obtain in Colorado because water storage is highly encouraged."

The property came with significant senior water rights on West Lake Creek, a claim first established by the original homesteaders in 1894. Under Kerwin's guidance, the Knapps re-established their priority rights on the Hawley-Reese irrigation ditch, originally dug by a homesteader in 1880, to convey six cubic feet per second (cfs) of water from a head gate located on West Lake Creek just south of the property line to three parcels at the head of the valley.

Guy Parker, the ranch manager and caretaker for the property at the time, was instrumental in re-establishing the ditch for the Knapps and the two adjacent neighbors, all of whom received a one-third share of the water. He recalls that the ditch was in complete disrepair due to a lack of ownership oversight. "Every spring, we would raise the headgate, and that water would race down the ditch at full speed. It never failed. A few days later, we would have a blow out somewhere along the line, and the water would pour down the hillside to the county road." One of Parker's first priorities was to install a twenty-four-inch pipe to convey the water from the headgate to the point where it diverts at the measurement point on the Knapps' property, a lengthy but worthwhile process that significantly reduced the annual ditch maintenance. Today, the Knapps' one-third share of water flows directly into the lake, where a portion of it is stored for fire protection, irrigation and trout fishing, and finally returned every twenty-seven days to the West Lake Creek system.

Water Rights in Colorado

In the late 1850s, following the California Gold Rush, many disappointed miners turned their eyes to Colorado, where gold was discovered near the present-day city of Denver in 1858-'59. They brought with them new ideas that had been developed in California to help settle conflicts over land and water use. The amount of Colorado's sporadic water supply that was available for use was heaven-sent, either arriving as runoff from heavy snows in the mountains or as later summer rainfall. Anything that fell from the sky in between those seasons was considered a bonus.

With minimal water available, very little land could be used for agricultural development. Panning for gold and growing basic crops near streams was a relatively simple endeavor, but as the population grew and technology developed, so did the need for a reliable water supply.

A water right is a right to use a predetermined portion of water, and every state has its own set of water laws. In Colorado, owning property that includes a section of a creek, stream or river does not automatically give the owner the right to use that water. Instead, as set forth in a series of laws related to water use and land ownership known as the Colorado Doctrine, all surface and groundwater in Colorado is a public resource to be used by public agencies and private citizens. Commonly referred to as "first in time, first in right" in periods of water shortage, this doctrine—which is administered by the Colorado Division of Water Resources—stipulates that the first person to appropriate water from a stream and put it to beneficial use on land has a legally protected property right to continue using that same amount of water, ahead of claims by other water users who hold junior water rights.

Obtaining a water right in Colorado is a complicated business, which requires the assistance of a water rights attorney and water engineer. The first step in the process involves the establishment of a plan of intent to divert water for beneficial use. This is followed by an application to the water court in the river basin in which the diversion exists. A court-appointed engineer reviews the application, and local water commissioners conduct field investigations. Any protests must be settled before a judge can sign a ruling and make it a decree of the court. A simple decree can take four months. More complicated cases may last anywhere from two to three years.

William Henry Jackson, History Colorado, #20103877

A photograph by William Henry Jackson, taken between 1886-1890, shows the confluence of Lake Creek and the Eagle River just below present-day Edwards.

Courtesy of Stream Team

A photographic montage from June 1990 shows the seasonal pond that appeared every spring in the glacially carved bowl just below the top of the hill at Knapp Ranch. This natural feature, formed thousands of years ago when the glacier halted its advance, was a collection point for spring runoff and excessive groundwater. An ecologically rich but temporary habitat for wildlife and birds, its presence provided the incentive to create a larger, more permanent lake environment.

Learning From Experts: The Lake—Building it Once, Filling it Twice

The job of transforming the sage-covered bowl into a lush lake environment fell to the Stream Team, a company run by the husband-and-wife duo of Jim and Susan Walsh, experts in lake and stream habitat construction. They went to work as soon as the snow started to melt, and with their transit and tape measure, they laid out the lake in a twenty-five-foot-square grid with lathe and flags. At the same time, they came up with the amount of water flow from the Hawley-Reese ditch water right needed to maximize the lake. This was a particularly important component of the lake design because of the potential for nutrient buildup, Jim Walsh explains. "At this altitude (nine thousand feet), even though the sun can penetrate fifteen to sixteen feet of water depth, unknown quantities of nutrients build up in the water. When you fill a pond or lake, those nutrients get chewed up and you get a bloom of blue-green algae." In order to avoid an algae bloom, a water body must be completely exchanged in a certain amount of time. "We came up with a certain amount of flow that allowed us to determine the size of the upper and lower lakes," Jim Walsh says. "The lower lake is three and a half surface acres with a maximum depth of seventeen to eighteen feet, with a percentage of shallows to deep, and mid-ranges to satisfy all of the habitat requirements of a viable and vibrant pond." At this size, the lake exchanges every twenty-seven days during the irrigation season, with water returning to West Lake Creek via underground pipe.

Not surprisingly, the geomorphology in this part of the country creates soil conditions that are highly variable, and potentially unstable. Sub-surface conditions in some areas are rocky and sandy; in other regions, heavy clay proliferates. At Knapp Ranch, layers of sand and clay coexist, creating a situation that proved particularly challenging in the construction of the lake.

Doug Lyle, owner of Left Hand Excavating in Longmont, Colorado, and his team had excavated the lake to a depth of fifteen feet when they discovered a dense, gray clay in the northeast quadrant of the lake. "It was as if the clay had been placed there in sheets," says Lyle. "We could pull it out in pieces, layer after layer."

"Water was seeping up through the clay and filling it up," recalls Jim Walsh. "The engineers looked at it and told us to cross our fingers because we might have uncovered a natural underground spring in the lake. On the other hand, they said it might have to do with a change in water pressure. Unfortunately, they were right. Once that lake was full, the water pressure changed, altering the inflow to an outflow. Seventeen feet of water suddenly drained out. That put a wrench in the process."

More likely, the water loss was due to the excavation of a thick lens of sand embedded between the layers of clay, a common—yet difficult—geologic condition to predict. Once the water found the sand, it simply followed the natural downhill course back to West Lake Creek.

Ultimately, the team drained the lake and began again. This time, however, they mixed in bentonite, a natural clay that is commonly used as a sealant in ponds and lakes due to its self-sealing and low-permeability features. The bentonite proved successful, and the lake has sustained its water level ever since.

Courtesy of Stream Team

The area where the lake now sits was once a grassy, moist meadow. The lake's size—about three and a half surface acres—was determined by the Knapps' water-right allotment from the Hawley-Reese ditch. Some of the water in the lake is retained for irrigation and fire protection needs, but the majority of it is returned to West Lake Creek via an underground pipe, located to the west of the Main Lodge on Knapp Ranch.

Courtesy of Stream Team

Courtesy of Stream Team

Courtesy of Stream Team

This page: The lake includes islands, shallow shelves, and inlets planted with native aspen and cottonwood trees, shrubs such as alder, ash, river birch, maple, red-twig dogwood, willow, and an array of wetland grasses, spike rush and sedge. Artificial reefs, also known as trout "condos," constructed from slabs of logs connected in a triangular shape, are anchored at the bottom of the lake, which is seventeen to eighteen feet deep. An aeration system ensures that both the vegetation and the fish population receive adequate oxygen and sunlight, particularly during the cold winter months.

Learning From Experts: Creating a Productive Fishery in the New Lake

Aquatic biologist Tami Schneck (owner of Aquatic Associates, based in Fort Collins, Colorado), agreed with the others about the potential for the development of a larger body of water in the naturally carved glacial bowl. She cautioned, however, that "you can't just dig a hole, fill it with water, and expect things to live there." A productive and healthy fishery needs three basic elements: cover, aquatic plants, and enough shallow area to support an insect population. The shallow, or littoral zone, supports the bugs and the forage fish, and provides shelter for hiding. Cover, in the form of overhanging rocks and shoreline vegetation, or submerged boulders and logs, provides refuge and spawning areas for fathead minnows, as well as some of the smaller trout. The woody debris of the logs also supplies a good substrate for insects. Submerged aquatic plants such as rushes, reeds and water iris help increase the nutrient base in the water while deterring more invasive species such as cattails, which, if left unattended, can become invasive, creating a virtual monoculture. Oxygen is the single most important water quality parameter for a healthy lake or pond. A proper aeration system circulates the water, pushing oxygen into the soil at the bottom of the lake, and maintaining the healthy bacteria that feeds the aquatic environment. Once the features and planting are in place, a natural food base is introduced to establish the food chain. Schneck used fathead minnows and a small freshwater shrimp called hyella at Knapp Ranch due to their ability to reproduce quickly in cold water.

In most newly developed lakes and ponds, lake stocking densities are kept fairly low, though once the system has stabilized, the numbers can increase. Today, the lake's target stocking density is one hundred fifty pounds per acre. Because trout do not reproduce successfully in still water, the population must be supplemented every two or three years. The fish are weighed and measured on a regular basis to make sure that the resource is not taxed.

Betsy Knapp

Once the lake was complete, the team introduced a variety of aquatic plants and fathead minnows, a forage fish that thrives in cold-water systems. Four species of trout—brown, rainbow, Snake River cutthroat, and brook—were introduced a few years later. And even though a lake of this size could sustain a stocking density of up to two hundred fifty pounds per acre, the team decided to cap it at one hundred fifty pounds to maintain a healthy system. Here, aquatic biologist Tami Schneck stocks the lake with trout of differing size and species.

Learning From Experts: Creating a Productive Fishery in the Creek

As the lake filled with water, the crew turned its attention to restoring the section of West Lake Creek that runs through the Knapp property. "This reach of the creek was a shallow and stagnant jumble of willow thickets, deadfall and beaver dams," says Schneck, describing its condition on her first visit to Knapp Ranch. Despite its appearance, Schneck was confident that it could be restored and become a viable resource.

Aquatic biologists like Schneck collect baseline data and provide technical input about existing conditions to stream restoration experts, who then use that information to design, restore, or construct a project. "Typically, our role is to define the existing resource and see what it will take to turn it into a better resource," she says. "I was invited to assess what is here, to look at the existing fishery and its limitations, to catalog the fish species and age classes, and complete a bug inventory."

The job of transforming the small section of West Lake Creek into an aesthetically pleasing and viable trout stream fell again to the Stream Team. Combining savvy engineering skills with shovels, handsaws and navigational tools, aquatic experts Susan and Jim Walsh began their quest to temper the stream and surrounding environs. "Sue and I set up a hand transit, and surveyed the entire stretch of West Lake Creek in twenty-foot increments," says Jim Walsh. "We took elevations, stream width, and center depths, and combined it with longitudinal profile. We had machetes and waders because everything was so overgrown. We moved that transit hundreds of times."

West Lake Creek's water was extraordinarily clear and clean. Unfortunately, it was too cold, and there were no nutrients in the system due to the substantial overgrowth and resulting lack of sunlight throughout the stream corridor. As soon as they removed the willow thickets, says Jim Walsh, the stream came to life. "Suddenly, the sunlight was hitting the stream and breaking through the decomposing elements where the macro invertebrates were living. The boulders and rocks became heat magnets, creating small microclimates. The bugs multiplied, and the trout responded!"

Betsy Knapp

A group watches as Tami Schneck and her crew weigh and measure the trout in West Lake Creek. Trout are cold-water fish whose presence usually indicates a healthy stream and watershed. Monitoring both the fish and their habitat on an annual basis is important for understanding temperature fluctuations, water quality, aquatic insect populations, stream habitat conditions, and vegetative cover.

A Lesson in Stream Restoration

Hydrologists categorize streams in a hierarchical order, ranging from one to twelve, based on whether they are perennial (consistent) or recurring (occasional). First- and second-order streams, also known as headwater streams, form in the steep upper reaches of mountainous areas, flowing quickly downward to meet a larger stream in the valley below. Fish and other aquatic species are few and far between—even in perennial first- and second-order streams, due to the steep and rocky terrain. But third order streams like West Lake Creek (which is also considered a headwater stream)—maintain an ecological richness that makes restoration a viable investment, if the owner is willing to go through the complex government permitting process required by the 1972 Federal Clean Water Act. Under Western water law, the U.S. Army Corps of Engineers issues that permit once the property owner has received approval from the local representative of the division of wildlife, the local water commissioner, the state historical society, and upstream and downstream neighbors.

Courtesy of Stream Team

Once the thicket of overgrown willow and deadfall was cleared away from the West Lake Creek channel, new vegetation species indigenous to the site were introduced to keep the stream bank from eroding. Typically, native plant species in riparian areas can restore themselves, but occasionally they need a jump-start. Here, workers plant willow plugs in the soft soil along the stream bank.

Betsy Knapp

Prior to commencing any work in a stream, river, or lake on private property, a landowner must receive approval from the U.S. Army Corps of Engineers, a process that can take several years to complete. It took two years for the Knapps to receive final approval to restore their section of West Lake Creek.

Soon after, excavator Doug Lyle began his work. An expert at his job, Lyle, shown here maneuvering a backhoe, assured the Knapps that if so much as a single drop of oil spilled from any of his equipment, he would discount his work significantly. Needless to say, his bills were paid in full.

Before-and-after photographs of West Lake Creek show the emergence of a "learn-to-fish" area on the grassy bank in the foreground of the lower photograph. Removing the willows made it possible for aspiring fishermen to practice casting in an area where their lines would not get tangled in vegetation.

Courtesy of Stream Team

The cold, clear water of West Lake Creek cascades over shallow riffles and boulders into deep pools, churning, grinding, and cleaning the water channel. Native willows, river birch, and alder line the banks, their arching branches providing protection for fish, birds, and other wildlife, while clearings in the trees introduce sunlight and heat, bringing with them a surplus of aquatic insects for bats, birds, and fish to feed on.

Learning From Experts: An Exercise in Site Planning

"When I was growing up, we would rent a house on an island off the coast of Maine that was only accessible by boat. There was something so immediate about living on a forested island surrounded on all sides by water, and I wanted to recreate some sense of that feeling here," says property owner Betsy Knapp. "When you live high in the Rocky Mountains with no ocean nearby, it's wonderful to be able to look outside and see water. The lake is very soothing."

Not surprisingly, re-creating an ideal like this in the arid high mountains of Colorado is the kind of project that can take decades. At the time the lake was finished, it looked very unnatural, says landscape architect Rick Lamb, adding that the house was the element that would ultimately secure its position within the upper valley. "There it was, a large body of water literally hanging in a bowl-shaped valley. What it needed was something large to anchor it in place." Typically, house and lake relationships are oriented hierarchically so that the house looks down upon the lake. But the Knapps, citing the Many Glacier Hotel in Glacier National Park as an example, wanted to locate the house in such a way that its ground-level line-of-sight with the lake was at eye level. In order to accomplish an on-grade sight-view plane, part of the foundational structure of the lodge was in fact a reinforced concrete dam meant to secure the separation of the Main Lodge from the lake waters.

© snehitdesign/www.fotosearch.com

The Many Glacier Hotel at Glacier National Park in northwest Montana was the inspiration for the siting of the Main Lodge. Here, Swiftcurrent Lake is at eye level with the central view. The lodge itself, large enough to match the oversized environment, maintains a profile that does not dominate the surrounding landscape.

Lamb's approach to planning and design at Knapp Ranch was greatly influenced by Frederick Law Olmsted's plan for Shelburne Farms in Shelburne, Vermont. Developed in 1886 as a model agricultural estate by members of the Vanderbilt family, Shelburne Farms includes four major buildings or barns that are clustered together in such a way that no single building penetrates the horizon from any point on the property. In similar fashion, Lamb reasoned, from no point on Knapp Ranch should a structure—no matter its size—break the horizon. More importantly, the house should fit into the landscape in such a way that it looked as if it had been there forever. "The whole idea of positioning the house for the Knapps was such that, as you came around the corner, the house—no matter the scale—would not counter the perspective and scale of the valley view. Rather, it would exist as a tranquil and special place unto itself," says Lamb. The Knapps agreed, pointing to examples of commercial and residential projects that have so obviously ignored their surroundings. "Rick's emphasis on ensuring that the house should fit the land—and not the other way around—was so insightful, educational and obvious," says Bud Knapp. "Before you decide to put your home at the top of the ridge so you get the best view, consider how you will live there. That location may give you superb views, but wind and sun exposure may make it impossible to be outside. When you look to the land for clues, important elements such as privacy and intimacy in your living space emerge, and ultimately you end up with a much more successful and livable plan."

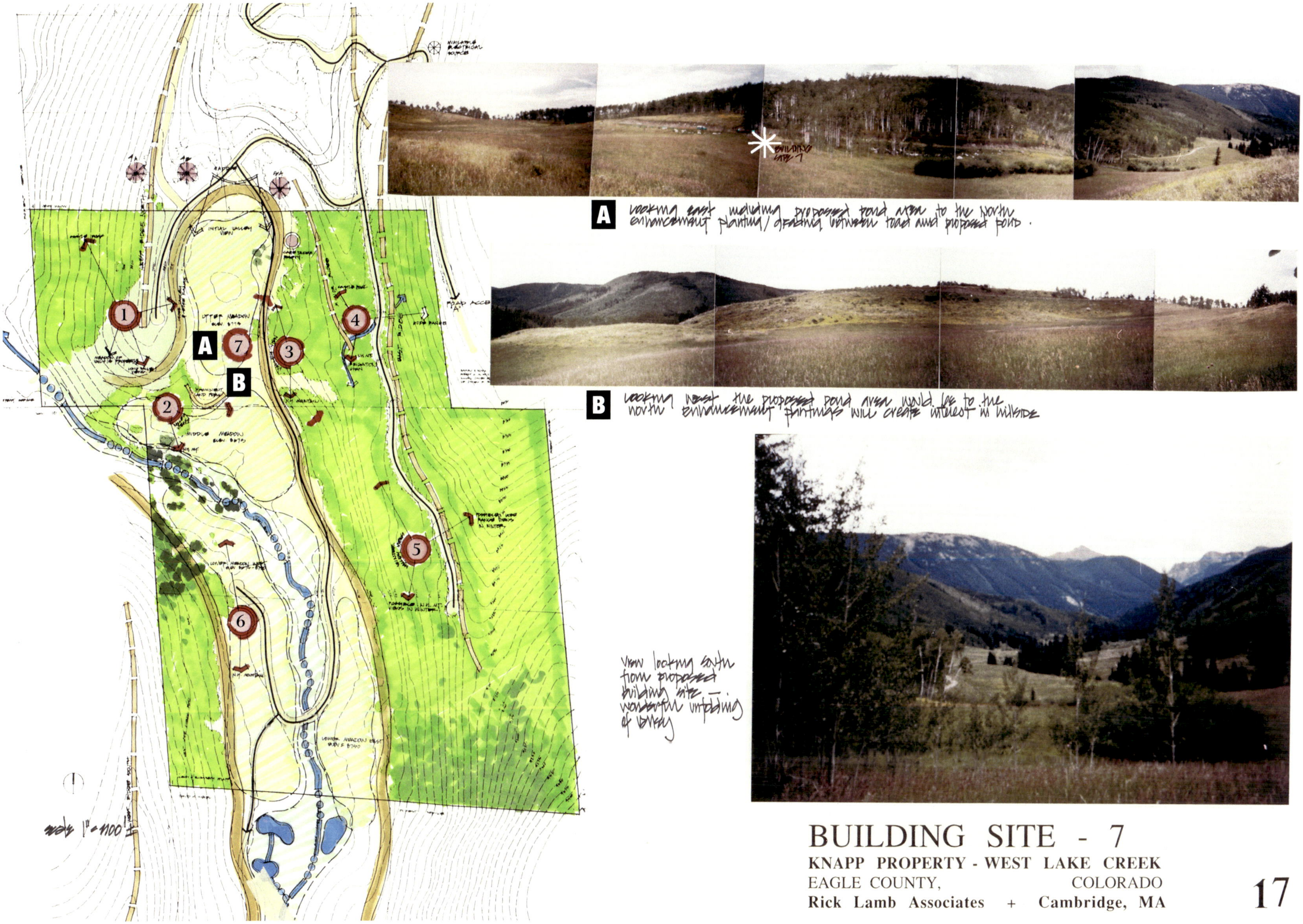

Courtesy of Rick Lamb

Landscape architect Rick Lamb's site analysis was used to determine a number of potential building sites on the property. After reviewing topographic features, slopes, drainage patterns, solar aspect, predominant wind direction and views, he recommended Site 7 as the best location for building the Main Lodge. Eventually, some of the remaining identified locations became the sites for the sawmill (5), The Farm at Knapp Ranch (6), and the caretaker's home (4). Photomontage A shows the location of Building Site 7. Montage B looks west over the proposed lake. All three photos on this page show what the valley looked like when the Knapps first visited.

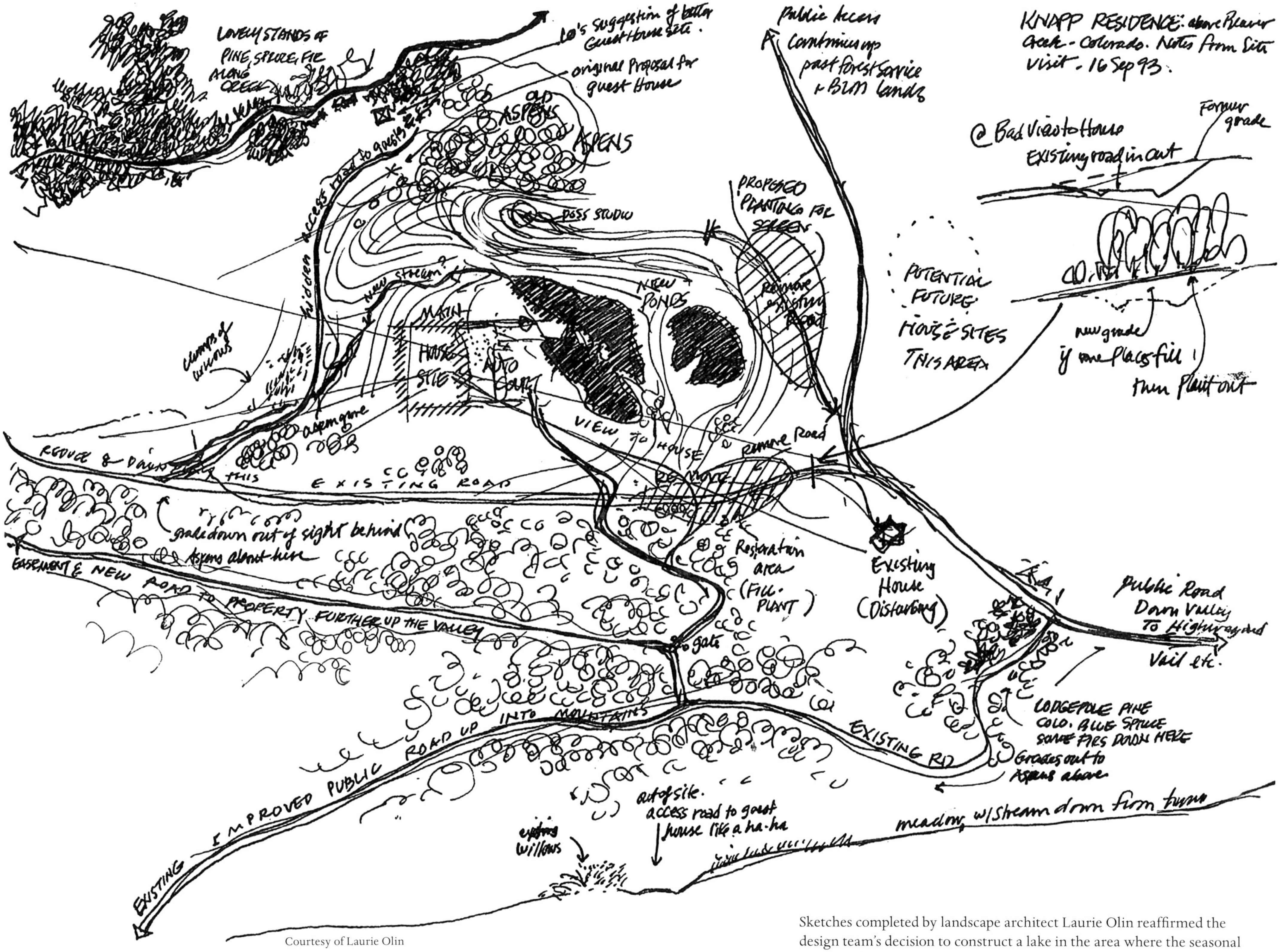

Courtesy of Laurie Olin

Sketches completed by landscape architect Laurie Olin reaffirmed the design team's decision to construct a lake in the area where the seasonal pond was located, and to establish a landscape that would look as if it had always been there.

Learning From Experts: "Don't mess it up."

In 1993, several years after Rick Lamb's initial site analysis had been completed, renowned landscape architect Laurie Olin visited the property at the behest of the architect to review and comment on the project and the ideas that were currently under development. "It's a great site and a great project," Olin concluded in his site observation report, cautioning the team to tread lightly on the land. "The principal landscape tasks here are those of accommodation and restoration. This is not a project crying out for landscape invention, for gardens and diversions, for lawns and floral displays. They would seem feeble and out of place. The principal task here is to keep from messing up a perfectly beautiful site, and to see to it that the new built elements fit in well."

The lake, originally considered just one feature in an already beautiful landscape, quickly became integral to the overall system. At three and a half surface acres in size, and about eighteen feet at its deepest point, the lake is an essential part of the natural environment, providing potable water for the Main Lodge and caretaker's home, and irrigation water, as well as supporting and regulating groundwater recharge, soil formation and biodiversity. It also serves as an immediate storage reservoir, in the event of a wildfire or period of drought. Visible from almost every room in the house, the lake attracts a variety of birds and wildlife throughout the year. Fishermen and boaters—even hardy swimmers—enjoy the opportunity to explore its depths, invigorating for the mind, the body, and the spirit.

Courtesy of Laurie Olin

© Charlie Summers/NPL/Minden Pictures

On the following pages, photographs illuminate the naturalness of the site. Native vegetation, introduced along the lake's edge, adds to the ecological diversity of the riparian environment, while the naturalized contours blend seamlessly into the existing topography.

Clockwise: Birds and insects, including dragonflies (*above left*), thrive in the deep vegetation along the lakeshore. A pair of Canada geese returns year after year to raise a family in the protective lake environment. Trout are often found hiding in the cool shade beneath the overhanging willows.

A great blue heron pauses while fishing for trout along the lake's shallow shoreline.

Twenty-five years after planting, the trees, shrubs and undergrowth are fully mature and thriving. Positioned in naturalistic groupings along the sloping lakeside and subject to plentiful water and sunlight, the vegetation has integrated almost seamlessly into the existing valley landscape.

I do not believe that any man can adequately appreciate the world of today unless he has some knowledge of—a little more than a slight knowledge, some feeling for and of—the history of the world of the past. —Teddy Roosevelt

3

METHOD

CRAFTING A STORY FOR OUR HOME

Montana Historical Society Research Center - Photograph Archives, Helena, Montana

Perched on the edge of a glacier-carved cirque, Glacier National Park's Sperry Chalet is a backcountry retreat built in 1914 by the Great Northern Railway in the style of luxury European hotels. From the Great Northern Railway (GNRy) letters on the gable to the roughened and irregular character of the stone walls, the chalet is an example of the coalescing of high alpine northern European and American architectural styles in a majestic American landscape. A National Historic Landmark, Sperry Chalet burned to the ground in a lightning-sparked wildfire in August 2017.

Historic Influences on Design Goals

In their 1974 book, *The Place of Houses*, architects Charles Moore, Gerald Allen, and Donlyn Lyndon suggest that the key to building a successful home lies in the kind of attention given to the way in which the house is constructed, and the way in which it helps focus or shape the lives of its residents. The project requires much more than just a financial investment, they say, noting that "care, liberated by knowledge and confidence and invested in a house, is an investment returnable with interest."

Armed with an innate thirst for knowledge and a desire to understand more about the process, Bud and Betsy Knapp began their own investigation into how they wanted their home to shape their lives. They began by carefully researching design and building concepts to find the ones best suited for their land, assembling photos and sketches that fit their general philosophy. "The value of pictures in a process like this can't be understated," says Bud Knapp, adding that he used to bristle when friends and acquaintances told him how useful his magazine *Architectural Digest* was, especially when they cut it up to show ideas to their architects or designers. "My first thought was always, 'How could you cut my magazine up?' Finally, I wised up and realized that, in fact, that's what this magazine is all about!"

In addition to combing specialty bookstores and libraries for books about architecture, the Knapps researched everything from the kinds of tools that homesteaders most likely used to build their cabins, to basic modern elements, such as electrical outlets and heat registers, stair risers, the R-value of window glass, electrical conduit, lightning rods, and cast-iron pipes. Reading Tracy Kidder's *House* helped them develop an architectural vocabulary, and at the same time, Betsy says, it encouraged them to fully engage in the challenging process of building a house on a piece of land that was miles away from the nearest paved road, power source, and sanitary sewer: "It helped us formulate questions about things that we take for granted in our personal space. What is the appropriate volume and scale for a structure in this landscape? And how can a home, designed to look one hundred years old, accommodate evolving technologies?"

Pragmatic, organized, and skilled at managing projects and working with people, the Knapps planned their home, describing their ideal as something "extraordinary, beautiful, [that would] naturally enhance the site. The 'look' we want to capture is a sense of timelessness; structures that appear to have been there for a hundred years and will last a hundred years [or] more" Betsy says. "The building design, craftsmanship, materials and site location must enhance the valley." What they wanted, in essence, was to create a building compound based on the handcrafted and rustic design of the northern European tradition, primarily as seen in the National Park Service's iconic "Parkitecture" style.

ur exploration of design ideas included a complete review of our library of Architectural Digest *issues, flagging images we liked, and noting why we liked them. Occasionally, we simply liked the composition. More often, materials, fenestration, indoor-outdoor relationship or the architecture caught our eye. We learned how to describe what we liked, and why. The fact that we could talk about it together resulted in a building program that we both agreed upon.* —Betsy Knapp

Photo by George Rose/Getty Images

Constructed of boulders and concrete in 1927, Gilbert Stanley Underwood's Ahwahnee Hotel (renamed the Majestic Yosemite Hotel in 2016) acknowledges the beauty of California's Yosemite Valley without trying to compete with it. Stone pillars built of native granite, combined with large sheets of glass, establish a natural relationship between the asymmetrical building and the rock formations that form the backdrop to its setting.

Parkitecture as the Unifying Architectural Element

In the early part of the twentieth century, the National Park Service perfected its own rustic architectural style. The Knapps researched this style, aptly named "Parkitecture," identifying the features in the lodges at Yellowstone, Yosemite, and Crater Lake that particularly appealed to them. In the foreword to the 1935 book, *Park Structures and Facilities,* the Park Service's chief architect at the time, Albert Good, urged builders to "resist the temptation to embellish nature's canvas." The most successful buildings, he writes, reflect a philosophy of moderation espoused by those designers who believe that "the success of [their] achievement is measurable by the yardstick of [their] self-restraint." The ideas in this book became guiding principles for the Knapps as they considered how to best integrate their project into the surrounding landscape—how to ensure that their settlement's materials, geometries, and scale coalesced with the subtleties of the upper West Lake Creek valley.

Parkitecture—also known as National Park Service Rustic—is the culmination of the National Park Service's desire to create buildings and facilities that harmonized with the natural environment, largely by avoiding any significant visual interruption of the natural and historic surroundings. Characterized by its extensive use of rudimentary tools and hand labor, Parkitecture rejected the regularity and symmetry of the industrial world, instead combining native wood and stone in the vernacular of the location to create visually appealing structures that appeared to grow out of the majestic landscapes in which they were located. The rustic style was applied to more than buildings; it inspired everything from picnic tables, dams, fences, restrooms and drinking fountains, to trail signs, lighting, storage sheds, bridges, and boathouses. The log cabin became a staple of Parkitecture because it epitomizes America's frontier spirit and the Western ideal of independence and simplicity.

True to their desire to embrace the past while engaging the future, the Knapps developed a comprehensive building program, outlining the architectural aesthetic they desired and detailing the way in which they would inhabit their home once it was completed. While many of those preliminary ideas were altered in the course of construction, the overarching design idea became the project's guiding light, directing everything else—including architectural details, landscape architecture, and interior design. In their written "Architectural Program," the Knapps describe the reasoning behind some of their specific architectural and programmatic details: *We are attracted to the architectural elements of the National Park Service structures as they were developed in the early 20th century (a blend of the Adirondack style and the Western style represented by the work done in Yellowstone and Yosemite). For us, this means a house that blends into the landscape, perhaps is built with logs and stone, has interior gathering spaces that are large and inviting, and captures the views of the lake and the mountains. We want each structure to represent timeless design with contemporary attention to energy efficiencies, design elements, materials, and features that we can expect with today's technology.*

—Knapp Property Architectural Program, August 30, 1992

In southern Oregon, Crater Lake Lodge sits on the rim overlooking the great volcanic caldera known as Crater Lake, located a thousand feet below. In a nod to its setting, the base of the predominantly wood-frame building consists of native rock. Topped with a steeply pitched roof to protect it from the region's heavy winter snowfall, the lodge blends almost seamlessly with its setting. Both Crater Lake Lodge and the Ahwahnee Hotel served as inspiration for the Knapps' Main Lodge.

Courtesy of Special Collections, UC Davis Library, Eastman Collection B-6307 D-51

Courtesy of Glacier Park Lodge, ca. 1936. Photographer T. J. Hileman

Left: Built in a traditional Swiss alpine chalet style, Glacier Park Lodge combines the elegance of northern European tradition with a grandeur that reflects America's Western landscape.

Courtesy of Lake McDonald Lodge, ca. 1920. Photographer R. E. 'Ted' Marble

Historic American Buildings Survey, Creator. *Lake Lodge, Southwest of Lake Junction, Lake, Teton County, WY.* Lake Teton County Wyoming, 1933. Library of Congress

Far left: Rustic architecture merges with a mountainous landscape at Glacier National Park's Lake McDonald Lodge.

Left: With its protruding overhang and rough-hewn logs, Yellowstone's Lake Lodge has a Western frontier sense of size and space.

Finding an Architect to Oversee the Design

When it came time to find an architect, the Knapps decided to conduct a two-phased competition, inviting six architects to visit the property and submit very basic schematic designs. "We gave each architect $1,000 and no requirements," says Bud Knapp. "We had the advantage of knowing how to work with creative people, and we were able to capitalize on both the extraordinary talent that we had assembled in this competition and the ideas that came about as a result. The person who doesn't know much about architecture and design probably would not have succeeded with such a process. When each of them saw the property and the portfolio of design ideas we had assembled, we hoped it would become clear to them the direction we wanted to go."

After they saw the initial presentations, the Knapps narrowed the field to three architects and asked them to present their ideas for the property. "We were interested in learning how each one would work with us, how they would respond to this environment, and how deep their experience and knowledge was of this high-altitude setting and its special climate challenges. We gained tremendous insight from the process, and many of the presentations gave us ideas for what we wanted to do here."

The original building program had called for a single-family home that included a number of guest rooms. But the resulting ideas ran the gamut from a tiered structure that resembled an 1890s mining-era building, to a compound of traditional log cabins, to a modern interpretation of a homesteader's cabin. The process confirmed for the Knapps what George Shaeffer of Shaeffer Construction had told them from the start: For the project to be a success, they needed an architect who was intimately familiar with designing for a mountain environment—including climate, aspect and slope, water, sunlight, and materials.

Ultimately, the Knapps chose Vail-based Gordon Pierce, AIA, an architect whose style resonated with their established program, and whose desire to incorporate local historic and natural elements outweighed his need to attach signature elements to the design.

Best known for cultivating an inspired European design ethic in Vail, Pierce arrived in Colorado in 1962 at the behest of his employer, Fitzhugh Scott, an original investor in, and architect of, what was to become Vail Resorts. Pierce was instrumental in the planning and design of Vail, imbuing it with the cozy feel of an alpine village. He did so by creating a pedestrian-oriented design that was groundbreaking for resort development at the time. Pierce's notion of a traditional mountain style is highly influenced by European architecture, particularly that of Germany, Austria, and Switzerland, with its use of wood, stone, deep overhangs and centrally placed open-hearth fireplaces, or inglenooks. For Pierce, quality, timelessness, and a sense of permanency are essential components of design.

Both Pierce's architectural style and his ability to forgo making a personal architectural statement resonated with the Knapps. As part-time residents of Vail for fifteen years, they had become fond of the village's traditional and charming European style. More importantly, however, they admired Pierce's design sensibility and his ability to understand both the site and the programmatic needs. In addition, Pierce was a proponent of employing local craftspeople. This idea was immediately appealing, and it became a major component of the building program. "One of the fundamental principles of this project," says Pierce, "was to provide a basic design framework that would then be worked out by artisans and craftsmen. It was only in the planning that my hand was on it, and in the orchestrating of the end results. What you see there today is the handiwork of a group of very talented and smart craftsmen and builders."

Courtesy of Gordon Pierce

Opposite: One of the first chalet-style homes architect Gordon Pierce designed in Vail reveals his affinity for incorporating elements of European alpine design, including battered foundation walls, deep overhangs, and steeply pitched roofs.

Above: Pierce's "napkin" sketches show the evolution of his creative design process and vision. His sketch for the MacPherson Cabin on Knapp Ranch, shown here, illustrates the way in which the building emerges organically from the ground around it. Pierce used this very tactile communication tool to identify and explain specific design elements and architectural details.

ESSAY

Designing with Nature

Gordon Pierce, AIA
Alamo, California

One of my first projects, not long after I graduated from the University of Illinois, involved the construction of a home in a rural area near Whitefish Bay, Wisconsin. It was a sunny day in late autumn of 1959 when I first visited the property with my new boss, Fitzhugh Scott, and another colleague from the firm. We found ourselves in a landscape straight out of a Wisconsin guidebook. Rolling hills and productive farmland dotted with fences, cows and an occasional row of corn stretched for as far as our eyes could see.

We had been there about five minutes when a pickup truck pulled up. In the bed of the truck was a living room couch. Without further elaboration, Fitz instructed my colleague and I to place the couch in a particular location in the field, and to have a seat. We placed the couch deep in the tall grass, and then lowered ourselves into its depths. All at once we were part of this place, our senses on overload with the sounds, smells, and sights of the vast prairie landscape surrounding us. Fitz told us to take note of how it felt to be consumed by a landscape of such extreme beauty and depth, because, he said, these are the ideas we need to keep in mind during every stage of the design process. From that moment, my design focus changed. No longer was I intent on creating "signature" buildings. Instead, I would design buildings that grow naturally from the land on which they sit. In other words, I made it my goal to create buildings that belong.

For more than fifty years as an architect, I have been fortunate to work in a range of climates and landscapes, from the humid jungles of the tropics, to the rugged and rocky terrain of the high mountains. Always, I carry with me the lesson of the "couch in the field" as a cornerstone of my design philosophy, and I continue to turn to nature to guide my design philosophy. Each project carries with it specific standards for success but always, the land is the golden thread that binds it all together. It's a process that requires listening, looking and questioning, but in the end, patience is rewarded with a project that stands the test of time.

From the beginning, the property owners, Betsy and Bud Knapp, made it clear that they had found a special place, and they did not want to mess it up. "The architecture," they wrote, "must be extraordinary, beautiful, and enhance the site. The look we want to capture is a sense of timelessness; structures should appear to have been there for a hundred years or more. The building design, materials, and site location must enhance the valley."

As I read the overview again and again, it occurred to me that beauty and timelessness are synonymous with nature's evolutionary cycles. The idea that the structures should appear well established, for "a hundred years or more," became the seed for my concept. This was a home with a history, and that history would be part of the design evolution.

To better acquaint myself with the site, I decided to undertake my own version of Fitzhugh Scott's couch experiment, spending a day and a night on the Knapp property. While sitting in front of my campfire under the stars, I began to muse about what it might have been like to have been there a hundred years ago. How would I have felt, and what would I have done? My daydream began to take shape with a story about a fictional character, and how he began to establish a place to live in the 1880s. I named him Adam Fisher—Adam, a reference to "man of the earth," and Fisher for the stream that runs through the property. Adam would have come from a somewhat prosperous family in England, which meant that he had a good education and enough money to survive, as well as a real and yet romantic sense of the land. He came to Colorado in search of gold, but instead fell in love with the valley he discovered. Putting myself in the mind of Adam, I decided that the first thing I would do is build a cabin. I would site it under a protective canopy of trees and close to water. This first cabin (now known as Silver Sal) is the smallest of the sod-roofed structures, and is located in the deep forest just above West Lake Creek.

The second thing I might do is write to my family back in England and invite them to join me in this new place. As the story unfolds, many of my relatives arrive, hailing from all parts of Great Britain. Together, we expand the small garden, plant an orchard and build a family compound adjacent to the lake that reflects our European heritage.

As I started to develop ways to bring the concept to reality in the late twentieth century, I realized, ironically, that there was no architect in this story. In fact, the original settlers had to have the carpentry and masonry skills needed to carry out such a project. Nature would put the finishing touches on the structures. As the architect, I was there to guide the process and ensure the concept as envisioned was delivered.

After I was commissioned to design the project, the story of Adam Fisher became a template that guided the design team in realizing the Knapps' vision. And while this fiction was somewhat akin to a Hans Christian Andersen fairy tale, it also gave way to the development of design ideas that were true to the times and not just a copy of details. Very quickly, the story became real for all of us.

The Knapp residence will always represent for me the idea that nature is—and should be—the primary consideration in any project. Nature decides how a building looks, how it is made, and how it functions. Native materials used in a thoughtful way can maximize a home's efficiency, durability, and sustainability. Such care also fosters stewardship and an appreciation for that place in which we choose to live. Ultimately, a successful design is one that takes its cues from the landscape around it. ◘

Betsy Knapp

Architect Gordon Pierce uses a draw knife to demonstrate the manner in which a rustic patina of tool marks should be applied to enrich the post, beams, and rafters in the Main Lodge on Knapp Ranch.

◦ Early Cabin Sketches ◦

© Gordon Pierce

In line with the National Park Service's design philosophy, the architectural plans at Knapp Ranch focused on harmonizing the built improvements with the natural setting, creating the illusion that the landscape had never actually been disturbed. These sketches, completed at design development stage, offer a more intimate look at the details of each type of log construction, demonstrating each cabin's ability to coalesce with the existing landscape.

© Gordon Pierce

A vignette of MacPherson Cabin's front door highlights the intimacy and comfort associated with a semi-enclosed entry, considered as both a transition space from the outdoors to the indoors, and as a welcoming environment in an otherwise primitive landscape.

A Story Emerges

Together, Pierce and the Knapps decided to use a fictionalized narrative of the valley's settlement—developed by members of the design team—to guide and inspire the design of the compound. Painting a picture of how the valley might have been settled, the story became a way for the team members to validate their design ideas, and elevate their collective levels of creativity and problem-solving. Everyone on the project got involved, putting their minds and bodies in the shoes of early settlers whose outlook on life and reasons for being here were very different from their own. In their determination to learn how buildings would have been constructed in central Colorado in the late 1880s, the Knapps did extensive research and encouraged their design team to do the same. Together, they poured over historic maps and photographs, rummaged libraries throughout the state for Western architecture and history books, and bounced around the rutted tracks of high mountain roads in search of old mining cabins.

From day one, Pierce urged the Knapps to consider the scale of their building. In a landscape as majestic as the valley, anything too small would seem like an afterthought, while a structure that was too large might appear bulky and unnatural. Locating the home high on the ridge above the valley—a common practice in mountainous environments—was unacceptable by these standards. "By the time I joined the team, the Knapps had identified six or seven locations for the main house," Pierce recalls. "We all kept returning to the place where the house is now located because it had the most comprehensive view. The idea of incorporating the long views to the mountains on one side, while engaging in a more intimate conversation with the lake appealed to all of us immensely. How extraordinary it would be to sit in the great room and take in a tremendous long view of the mountains to one side while maintaining eye level with the lake to the other."

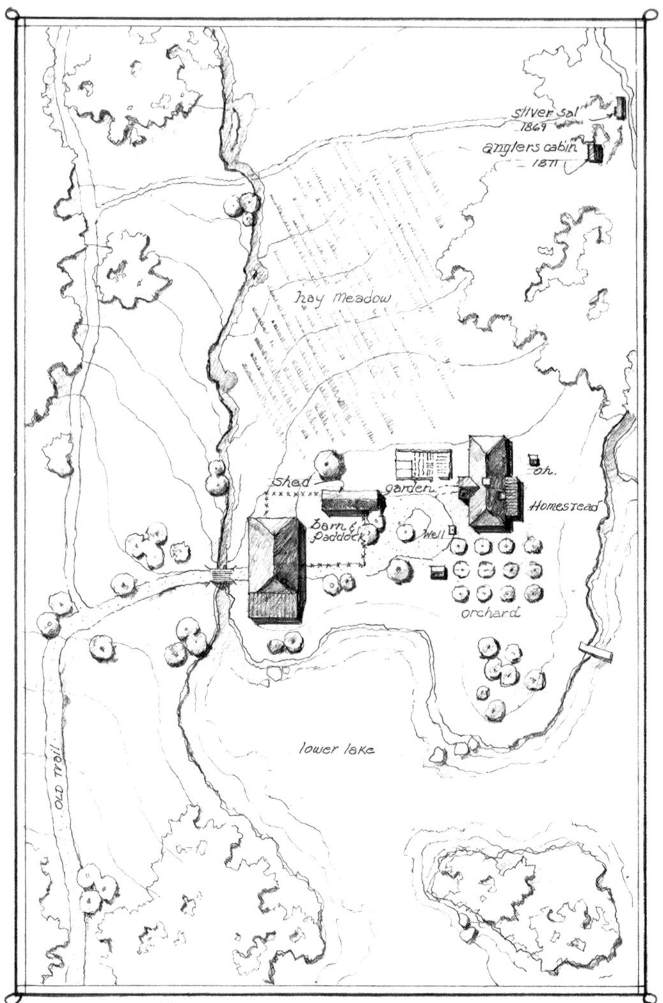

Homestead 1873 - 74

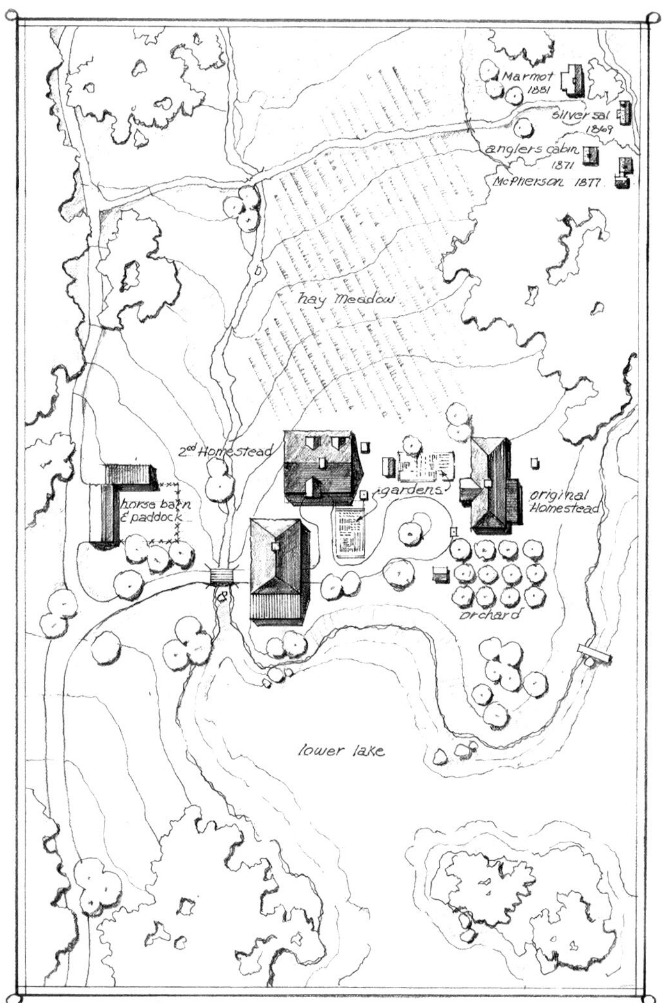

Homestead 1892

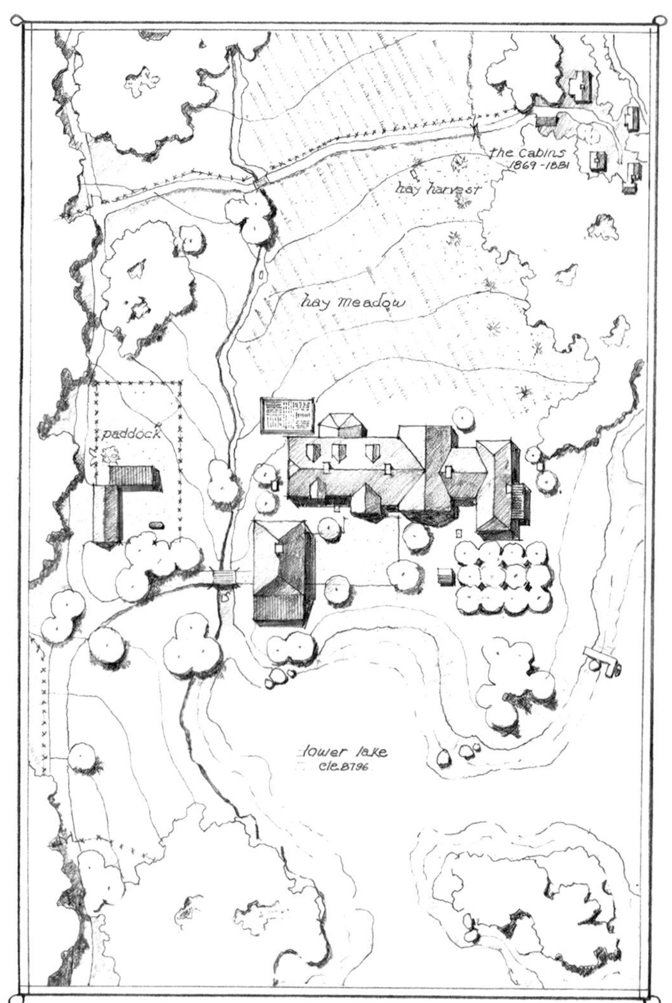

Homestead 1910

© Gordon Pierce

One of Pierce's immediate challenges was the creation of a building compound that would separate guest cabins from the main residence in a manner that fostered a sense of privacy and intimacy while encouraging guests to interact with one another and the surrounding environment. Recalling again her visits to the island in Maine, Betsy Knapp describes the feeling of staying in a remote cabin in the forest that was connected by boardwalk to other cabins: "Imagine an island without cars, where guests had to haul their belongings in little red wagons. It was a remarkable place for a ten-year-old to grow up." That adventure was followed by a summer family foray to Phantom Valley Ranch, a dude ranch in northern Colorado. Betsy has fond memories of group dinners in the centrally located main lodge. "I was particularly intrigued with the idea of creating a central space for conversation and shared meals," she says. "For me, that ranch experience was the perfect model of what we were trying to create here: an atmosphere of stimulation and camaraderie amongst family and friends. We liked the idea that guests could retreat to their individual cabins, tucked in the trees, for rest and relaxation, but if they wanted to eat, they had to join with others in a central location."

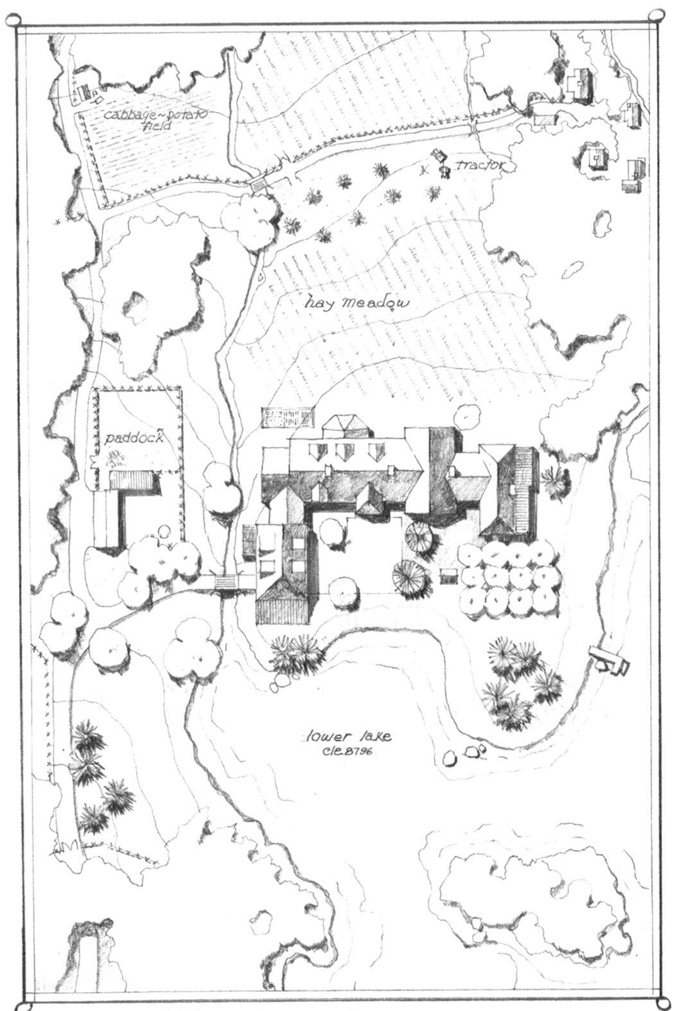

Homestead 1921~1935

Pierce was very open to the idea, particularly because the concept fit so well with the design team's fictional narrative about how the valley was settled. "I felt that breaking the program into a compound of buildings was completely believable," he says. "My thought was that when the first settler arrived in this valley, he just fell in love with it, building himself a rudimentary cabin, which turns out to be the littlest cabin, Silver Sal, named in honor of Bud's mother, Sally Knapp, and the silver mining nearby. Following the storyline, various family members arrived soon after, building their own cabins and ultimately creating the compound that exists here now, which includes the main house and four cabins—Marmot Guest Lodge, Silver Sal, MacPherson (named for Betsy's family) and Anglers."

These four drawings illustrate the evolution of the Main Lodge as it might have transitioned from a one-room homestead in 1873 to a complex compound of connected buildings in 1935. The original log cabin and barn (now the master bedroom and caretaker's quarters) would have been built in 1873 by the homesteader's brother, a man with a family, a few cows and sheep, and a need for more space. As the family grew in size and wealth, they filled in the space between the two buildings with a more modern Colorado farmhouse, complete with a kitchen and dining room. In 1910, this imaginary family returned to England, eager to show off their newly acquired wealth and "American" ways. During their visit, they became intrigued by the integration of light and space they observed in Europe's finest cathedrals. When they returned to West Lake Creek, they incorporated those ideas of light and space in a grand two-story, timber-frame living room, complete with large picture windows, a central inglenook fireplace, and a formal front door and entry area. Finally, around 1935, the buildings, which would have been constructed at different times over a period of sixty years, were joined together. By then, the orchard and gardens were well established and productive, and the family would have expanded to include multiple generations. "These may be fictional characters," Betsy Knapp acknowledges, "but their story echoes that of every other settler in this region. Their history is celebrated in a series of buildings that pay homage to the truly gifted craftsmanship of the time."

Authentic Expressions in Interior Design

In a process similar to the one they used to select an architect, the Knapps held an interior design competition, inviting six designers to present ideas. Again, the ideas were varied, ranging from a traditional rustic mountain aesthetic to a more modern style that integrated antiques from the Knapps' collection with one-of-a-kind handcrafted pieces reflecting elements of the surrounding natural environment. Ultimately, they chose Denver-based Associates III, a firm that had distinguished itself by its distinctive sustainable design philosophy, as well as its willingness to work within the parameters of the Knapps' existing collection of fine art, American Indian artifacts, family heirlooms and unique pieces of furniture.

Associates III principals Kari Foster, AID, and Annette Stelmack, AID, regarded the creation of an environment of authenticity as their ultimate goal. Says Stelmack, "Every single decision was authentic and meaningful—even down to the cushions with tape on them! Nothing was done just because it was pretty, or we thought it would look nice together. We were forever mindful of how it would fit into the narrative, and how it would have been done at that given point in time."

Green building and sustainable design are concepts that grew out of the need and desire for more energy-efficient and environmentally friendly building practices. In the twenty-first century, new technologies are constantly being developed to create greener structures. Even back in the 1980s, however, those at the forefront of their professions recognized the importance of reducing the impact of development on human health and the natural environment. Associates III was one of the first interior design firms to apply sustainable building practices in interior design, and the designers there expanded their role as environmental advocates through a book, appropriately titled *Sustainable Residential Interiors*, a publication that is now the go-to resource for reference material on topics ranging from indoor air quality to conserving energy and water.

Foster, founder of the firm and lead designer, says, "We always sold quality furniture and built things that were durable, long-lasting, and local (before local was cool). We did it because it was the right way to do it, not because we thought we could gain clients or awards by doing it. What has come out of it, some thirty-five years later, is a methodology that is almost secondary to our design process now. All of us are engaged in sustainable design, from ridding ourselves of toxic chemicals under our sinks, to testing the paint that is on our walls, to working with local artists and craftspeople."

With the addition of Foster and Stelmack, the team was complete. From the very beginning it showed the kind of esprit de corps that only comes from mutual respect and a willingness to laugh, admit mistakes, and look to fellow teammates for inspiration and humor. Bud Knapp made it clear early on that he didn't want any prima donnas on the project. "He wanted a team that could work well together and that could create a final product that looked like no architect or designer had touched it," Foster recalls. "Because of that, we were all able to come from a humble place."

One of the main tenets of the building program was to engage artists and craftsmen in all aspects of design and construction. Bud credits mentors from early in his career at *Architectural Digest* for opening his eyes to the value of handmade things. That laid the foundation for this project. "We wanted to engage people who knew how to make things by hand," Bud Knapp says. "Sure, we knew it would be more expensive, but it was certainly worth the premium."

Having worked extensively with creative people, the Knapps both understood and respected the creative process, making it clear to the team from the beginning that they would not be allowed to dictate anyone's final product. The rare gift of time, space, and the freedom to explore ideas would, they thought, encourage people to produce their finest work. Pointing to the stone on the fireplace in the Main Lodge, Bud describes how he and Gerald Gallegos, founder of The Gallegos Corporation, came to agree on what kind of stone to use: "When I told him that I wanted it to look like we had just gathered it up out of the field, he said, 'Get in the car and let's drive somewhere.' We drove to a quarry site where he pointed to a mound of rubble in front of us and said, 'We'll harvest it from that pile.' 'You don't care about size or shape or color?' I replied, 'No, because your process is genuine. You're doing what original settlers did years ago.'"

"This project was about authenticity," adds Foster. "It was about using reclaimed wood and pavers, engaging the old methods of joinery, and using local craftsmen." Stepping back in time was a huge challenge for the craftspeople, yet most of them have good memories of this project for the simple reason that they felt valued and respected for their skill and opinions.

"We made up stories for the workers so they could put themselves in the position of understanding who was building this house," Foster continues. "That elicited a lot of pride, particularly among the masons. They enjoy working on any beautiful home, but here, they were respected. The craftspeople became the number-one contributors to this project, and they so filled those shoes."

Stelmack concurs: "This was not about ego design. To have a project where craftsmanship is so revered is very unusual, and Bud set that up from the beginning. There were times when Kari and I would stand by and watch as credit for something we had designed was given to a craftsperson. Bud would point to us or Gordon and say, 'These people are not the important people on the project.' And then he would point to the stonemason or woodworker and say, 'This is the important person on the project. This is who builds this project.' I loved that piece because there was such a respect for craft and land, and doing things from the heart."

Andy Romero of The Gallegos Corporation recalls fondly the high morale on the site: "Even though most of my crew was Spanish-speaking, Bud would always look at them and give them a thumbs-up or pat them on the back. He couldn't have a conversation with them, but you could see it in their eyes that they wanted to do a good job. They were proud of their work, and because he acknowledged them, they wanted to do a better job."

Designing a home should be a pleasure, but endless decisions and tight timeframes often disrupt the process, pitting team members against one another. In this case, however, the team was able to follow architect Gordon Pierce's basic roadmap while being encouraged to come up with their own solutions to problems. Pierce's associate, architect Larry Deckard, AIA, brought an appreciable talent for translating big ideas into workable solutions. Never far from the site, Deckard could troubleshoot almost anything, and was available to answer questions from anyone working on the project. Foster and Stelmack embraced the historical context of the design, investigating everything from metalwork and door hardware, to light fixtures, fabrics, fenestration, and fireplace doors. They drew upon this research to create theme books for each building and prepare full-scale schematic mock-ups of finishes, fabrics, and furniture. Both women agree that collaborative teamwork was essential to the project's success, citing specifically the challenges inherent in melding the powerful masculine elements found in the rough-hewn exterior materials with the more welcoming feminine features of the interiors. "While men were integral to the creation of the structure and architectural elements instilling strength, pioneering spirit and a sense of protection," says Foster, "the women were integral to its softening by conveying warmth, comfort, and playfulness into the living spaces. The creation of a home is best when there is integration of both the masculine and feminine, creating a sense of deep well-being and balance."

Courtesy of Donna Barta Winfield © Associates III Inc.

Courtesy of Donna Barta Winfield © Associates III Inc.

The intimacy and playfulness of a kitchen *(left)* and bathroom *(above)* are visible in these schematic sketches. Interior spaces were carefully conceived to combine and balance the elements of strength and warmth, creating living areas that are both authentic and comforting.

Drawings courtesy of Rudi Neumayr

Austrian woodcrafter Rudi Neumayr's drawings convey the rich spirit of the European wood tradition that comes alive in his designs. Every door, cabinet, hinge, and wood detail was carefully designed and executed to reflect the individuality and functionality of each space.

ESSAY

A Legacy for Future Generations

Kari Foster, Principal, Associates III Interior Design
Denver, Colorado

Courtesy of Marianne Martin, Real Life Portraits

Associates III Interior Design had been creating interior design for mountain homes, ranches and resorts for a number of years when we were invited to interview for the Knapp Ranch project. One of our interviews included a shared meal on the property, where we were captivated by the grandeur of the setting. That day, while basking in the sweetness of an old-fashioned picnic, cradled within the intimacy of a verdant mountain meadow, we first experienced the essence of the Rocky Mountain magic of this magnificent place.

We were thrilled beyond measure to be chosen for the project, and we put our heart and soul into the undertaking. Bud and Betsy Knapp trusted us with their dreams for a family retreat, a place of renewal, an escape from the bustle of the city where they could enjoy true living. For us, it was the opportunity of a lifetime to bring the ranch buildings to life, and to aid Bud and Betsy with the creation of their vision for this pristine—almost sacred—site. The stream had been restored, the lake was in place, the saga for the buildings had been penned, and it was time to bring the structures alive with the comfort of home.

Authenticity was paramount as our design team adhered to the goal of individuality for each building. Our task was to express this uniqueness in the interior architecture and to provide careful detailing of the millwork, finishes, light fixtures, furnishings, fabrics, artwork, and accessories.

Our charge from Bud and Betsy Knapp, the property owners: to work in such a way that when our task was complete, it would appear as though no interior designer had ever set foot on the property. Our challenge was to create a place as honest and as natural as the land itself, true to those who had settled there previously. The stone should look as though an early settler had hastily assembled boulders found on the land to form a foundation, with timbers joined to provide a solid structure. It should demonstrate a primitive quality, without the slick appearance of a more polished urban structure. Bud and Betsy granted us ample time to get to know the land, learn from the team, communicate with each other, and to ensure that each voice was heard. We were given the freedom and the gift of time to do our very best work. The team in its entirety was collaborative from day one; weekly meetings took place throughout the interior construction of the project, ensuring organization, collaboration, attention to detail, time to ruminate, to question, and to guarantee authenticity. Bud and Betsy empowered us by giving us respect, encouragement, and trust. They were with us as wise guides every step of the way.

We accepted the challenge and freedom we were given to research materials that were used in times of yore, poring through numerous books and images. Stirred by the past, we rounded up inspirational images and hit our sketchpads. We selected woods that were reclaimed, designed doors and light fixtures from solid, simple materials, and searched for vintage tubs, and primitive fixtures and fittings. Sometimes, at Betsy's request, we added a modern touch, such as glass shower doors, figuring that now and then the fictional new owners would have wanted an extravagance of that nature, prompted by sights glimpsed on their forays to the eastern U.S. and Europe. Environmental goals were achieved through the use of reclaimed woods, low VOC adhesives and water-based finishes, longer-life, durable and locally sourced materials, and Energy Star appliances.

Bud said more than once that it was the craftsmen who were the keys to the project. We needed to bring our best talents, but check our egos at the door. Once we settled on a design, we tracked down the particular artisans equipped to aid us in exquisitely crafting every facet of the interiors. One of the project's most challenging aspects, for example, was figuring out how to encourage the stonemasons and the wood craftsmen to be more elementary—to be less meticulous in the way one stone was placed next to its neighbor on a fireplace and to leave more space; to allow for a slightly uneven plank on the floor, to ensure that as you walked from one era of the Main Lodge to another, there was an ever so slight variation in the elevation you were walking across, as though the home had naturally settled over time.

Remnants of the past are visible everywhere. Stone walls and stone floors in the wine room are warmed by rescued wine-cask wood planking on the ceiling—the scent of red wine emanating from the wood. There's also an antique claw-footed tub and original porcelain vanities in bathrooms. The furniture is primarily collectibles for case goods, rugs, lighting, and accent pieces. Together with Betsy, we combed antique stores in Colorado and along the Eastern Seaboard for rustic, yet lovingly and artfully assembled case pieces. When reproductions were necessary, we committed to using reclaimed woods, while custom soft goods were manufactured locally using antique and natural pre-washed fabrics, quilts, and blankets. Blending the rusticity and elegance of the past, they are true to their roots and the era.

In the end, one of the best compliments we received came whenever visitors asked how long ago the lodge and cabins had been built. The authenticity and historical accuracy we had all worked so hard to achieve was evident. It embraced the owners' dream of providing a place that was both reminiscent of the past, and open to the hope and spirit of the future. ◻

Courtesy of Annette Stelmack © Associates III Inc.

High in the mountains stands a legacy for future generations, a home that treads lightly on the land where guests experience the natural environment in a rare setting. —Kari Foster

Barely visible under a light dusting of snow and autumn leaves, Marmot Bridge floats above West Lake Creek.

Introducing Character Elements in the Landscape

Landscape architect Rick Lamb set the stage for the creation of a living environment in which water, mountain views, and human comfort amid the varied climatic conditions of a high mountain valley prevailed. As the design of the Main Lodge and cabins progressed, Jim Hyatt and Chris Olsen of the landscape architecture firm EDAW continued where Lamb left off. Working closely with the architects, Hyatt and Olsen were instrumental in ensuring that each building settled into the landscape in such a way that it looked as if it had been there for decades. In areas where vegetation was sparse, they brought in mature native spruce and aspen. Patches of weeds and hard-packed gravelly soil, left over from years of construction and speculation, were replaced with a native high-mountain-meadow mix of grasses and wildflowers. Aspen trees, planted in random clusters, were placed on both sides of the county road, effectively bringing the forest edge closer to the valley floor. Cottonwood trees, interspersed with aspen, spruce and willow, were planted around the lake. In areas where ground and surface water remains plentiful, those trees have assimilated so completely that the lake now looks as if it has been there forever.

Betsy Knapp

The landscape architects took their cue from the National Park Service's "Parkitecture" style, designing and siting structures built from native logs and rock that would blend—almost seamlessly—with the surrounding environment. Here, property managers Guy Parker (left) and Tony Ryerson (right), help set the Marmot Bridge in place over West Lake Creek.

The landscape architects also created a system of naturalized trails that wind sinuously through the forest, connecting the cabins to the Main Lodge. Farther afield, the trails detour at destinations along both sides of West Lake Creek and the lower meadows. Throughout the property, rustic bridges, fences, signs, and other structures, all designed and built in the Parkitecture style, blend almost imperceptibly into the landscape. Olsen and Hyatt's creative juices flourished during this time, and their brainstorming sessions were far-ranging and fruitful. "The Knapps encouraged us to develop our concepts, to go wild and think of everything," says Hyatt, even though many of the ideas—a screened-in "napping station" up in the aspens, a cross-country warming hut in the meadow, a playground and a ceremonial fire pit—were never realized. "We used a lot of character elements from the 1930s National Park Service books, and because there were so many talented craftspeople working here at the time, we could give our sketches to one of the log guys, and they would build it on the spot."

"Betsy and Bud were trying to create a wonderful place to live and a beautiful thing for the future … something that would last," says longtime friend and advisor Steve Cranston. "We take that stuff for granted now because everything has to be 'green.' They were doing cutting-edge stuff then. They wanted everything to be nice and as much a part of the environment as it was when they arrived." Photographer and friend Jim McHugh, agrees. "Betsy and Bud don't have a need to show off the architecture. Those buildings aren't lit by spotlights at night. They are simply happy to know that they are there. Allowing them to blend into the landscape and not disturb the natural surroundings reflects a deeper purpose, one that is about respect for the surrounding environment and those that were here before."

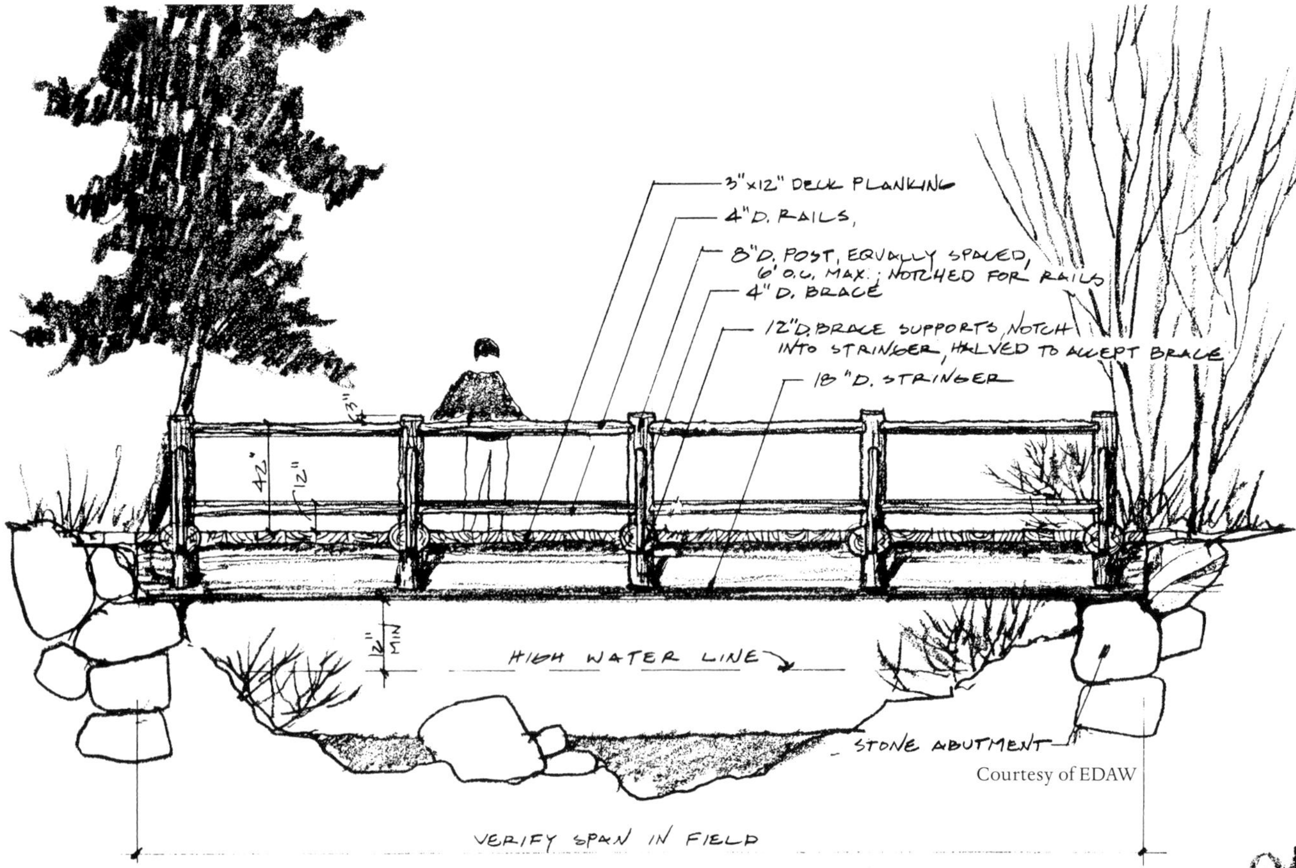

Courtesy of EDAW

The landscape architects gave sketches of Marmot Bridge *(top)* and Cathedral Bridge (*right*) to the log and stone craftsmen to assist them in construction. Both the drawings here and the photographs on the following pages reveal the underlying concept: that design should mimic nature. In most cases, the designers' drawings were creatively adapted to the individual site conditions.

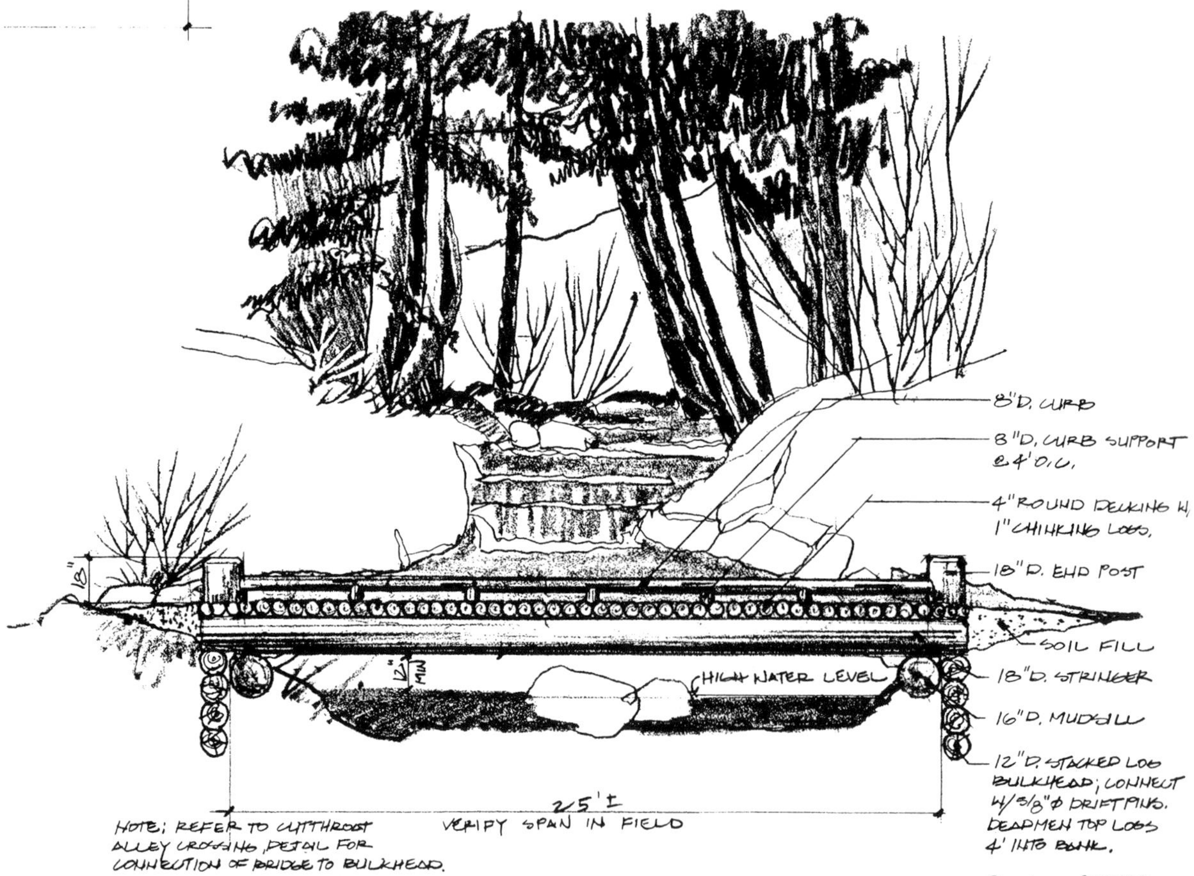

Courtesy of EDAW

A simple two-track gravel lane winds through the forest toward the cabins. Edged with native grass and a rustic three-rail fence made from aspen harvested on the property, the tracks all but disappear into the existing landscape.

An elevated walkway connects Marmot Lodge and the top of the slope with the creek below. Constructed from similar-sized lodgepole pine logs from the surrounding forest, the walkway appears as an organic extension of the columnar tree trunks through which it passes.

Simple cross planks are placed along both banks of West Lake Creek, facilitating ease of access when crossing wet areas.

We need some contact with the things we sprang from. We need nature at least as a part of the context of our lives. Without cities we cannot be civilized. Without nature, without wilderness even, we are compelled to renounce an important part of our heritage. —Joseph Wood Krutch

The term 'rustic' should mean more than the worn and misused term implies. Successfully handled, it is a style which, through the use of native materials in proper scale, and through the avoidance of rigid, straight lines, and over-sophistication, gives the feeling of having been executed by pioneer craftsmen with limited hand tools. It achieves sympathy with natural surroundings and with the past. Rustic can also be synonymous with 'pioneer.' —*Apologia*, National Park Service, 1935.

4

ASSEMBLY

INTEGRATING PAST, PRESENT AND FUTURE

Homesteading in the Mountains

In nineteenth- and early twentieth-century Colorado, gold and silver mining was the most significant industry, and it is most likely responsible for bringing about the social, economic, and political changes that ultimately led to Colorado achieving statehood in 1876. Over a period of fifty years, thousands of people surged into the region, seeking their fortunes in an unforgiving natural environment that few were prepared for. Many of them found the hardships too daunting, and gave up on Colorado altogether. But others simply repacked their tents, tools and bedrolls, and piled their trunks, furniture, cast-iron skillets and other useful items onto wagons, and set out for greener pastures in the high country. Traveling through the dense conifer forests and broad grassy parks of the "Shining Mountains," they discovered hidden valleys, abundant water, and warmer locales in which to settle into a quieter agricultural lifestyle. The early homesteaders in upper Lake Creek must have breathed a collective sigh of relief upon discovering this valley. Here was a place they could finally call home, a place where they were protected from the elements, where water, tillable land, healthy forests, and wild game were abundant.

The more typical American log structures—buildings defined by board-on-board and log construction—protected the newly arrived families from weather and wild animals. Constructing them was simple; no nails were needed, and the settlers used readily available materials, shaped with the basic pioneer tools—the ax, adze, and drill. Their structures required no written plans and could be modified for use as dwellings for humans or animals, or made into smaller outbuildings like smokehouses or granaries. Most cabins in the Rocky Mountains were simple one-room structures, crudely constructed from local logs and stone. Stone fireplaces and woodstoves kept the cabins warm throughout the winter, while deep porches enabled the family to escape the tight cabin quarters during the warmer months. In the summer, beds, chairs, and even the dining room table were often moved outside under the protective covering of the heavy overhangs. New arrivals and relatives from other parts of America and Europe brought knowledge of advanced construction techniques and more modern materials. When the Denver and Rio Grande Railroad reached Edwards in 1887, it brought more fragile goods such as furniture and glass—items that previously had to be carried over rugged land on the back of a horse or a mule.

Lake Creek became a close-knit community formed by individuals and families who staked their ground here to create a new life in a new country. Legally, economically, and even historically bound to the land they owned, these people maintained strong ties with one another, deferring to the sense of neighborliness that comes from living in an environment of extremes.

Signs of this unique and regional history are visible everywhere at Knapp Ranch: in the genius of design, the creativity of the details and craftsmanship, in the intelligence of the construction, and in the siting of structures within the greater landscape. The architecture and land-use patterns speak of a respect for place, people and history, a commingling of past, present, and future. The beautifully wild natural environment is only enhanced by carefully conceived elements, whose subtle placement belies the presence of the human hand. Together, these pieces form a pattern language that highlights the power of creative collaboration, coupled with a desire to create a compound of buildings that interpret history in a simple but comfortable, even refined and elegant, way. Beautiful cabins with roughened, irregular stone foundations appear to spring naturally from the ground, their rugged proportions almost disappearing into the natural setting.

Courtesy of Eagle County Historical Society, Eagle Valley Library District

An original log homestead in Beaver Creek, c. 1895-1910. In her book, *The First Pioneers: A Squaw Creek History*, Vail author June Simonton described the communal camaraderie that existed for these early settlers. "They [the pioneers] lived on the satisfactions of building their own homes on their own land, the pleasures of family talk, first seeds sprouting in early summer, the hard work of harvest, dances at the schoolhouse, a picnic under the spruces—the gatherings of young and old over all those years to celebrate their life in a high, clean Colorado valley."

Buildings Rooted in Northern European Tradition

Historians speculate that log structures first appeared in northern Europe during the Bronze Age (about 3500 BC), spawning a building tradition that became popular in the Scandinavian countries, Germany, and northern Russia, where the large native stands of softwood timber could easily be manipulated with simple hand tools. In eighteenth- and nineteenth-century America, the log cabin style became the primary mode of construction for pioneers and settlers. Hand tools were easy to transport; all the settlers needed were dense forests and strong bodies. Most log cabins consisted of a single room with a door; windows were cut into the walls, covered with animal skins or boards fixed to slide across the openings. A fireplace, located at one end of the room, provided light, warmth, and a place to cook. Walls were chinked with mud, cloth, animal droppings, or newspaper, and most floors consisted of tamped-down earth.

Many cabins, hastily constructed to provide immediate shelter for restless wanderers, disintegrated almost as quickly as they were built. Other cabins employed a level of detail that suggest a more permanent settlement. Pioneer settlers who preferred flat walls to rounded ones used hand-hewn logs for building. Not only did these hewn logs give their dwellings a more traditional appearance, the flat walls were better able to withstand the elements, as the process of hewing the logs removed the bark and other decayed exterior wood.

The log cabin style eventually became synonymous with "the good life," particularly in parts of the country where enclaves of wealthy industrialists sought to escape the heat and stench of the densely populated eastern cities for a life of fresh air and simplicity. The Great Camps of the Adirondacks are one example of log structures designed to satisfy nostalgia for a simpler life. Later, architects of national park structures such as Yellowstone's Old Faithful Inn revived the log cabin aesthetic in an attempt to blend buildings with their surroundings. In addition, the Civilian Conservation Corps (CCC) worked with the National Park Service and the U.S. Forest Service during the Great Depression of the 1930s to build thousands of log structures in the national forests and parks. Ultimately, the CCC helped to preserve the log cabin tradition and promote a self-sufficient lifestyle that has continued to develop in a myriad of ways in the twentieth and early twenty-first centuries.

Courtesy of Eagle County Historical Society, Eagle Valley Library District

Created to address national conservation needs as well as unemployment, the Civilian Conservation Corps (CCC) devoted much of its labor to the national forests, where teams of workers were responsible for building restrooms, walls, lookout towers, and bridges. Here, young men from the CCC lay a stone foundation wall for the Tigiwon Camp Community House in nearby Minturn, Colorado, in Holy Cross National Forest, now known as the White River National Forest, c. 1931-1934.

Hand-crafted Cabins

Because log construction does not require a lot of tools, it has an advantage over other types of construction. In fact, most log cabins could be raised and largely completed with as few as two to four different tools—including a felling ax, a broad ax, and a handsaw or crosscut saw. A felling ax was typically used for bringing down a tree and cutting the logs to the appropriate length. Round logs were hewn flat with a broad ax, or more finely finished with an adze as smooth thick planks. Notching was done with an ax, hatchet, or crosscut saw; openings for doors and windows were usually cut after the logs were set into place, and door and window frames, particularly jambs, were inserted during construction to help hold the logs in place. Roof-framing members and floor joists were either hewn from logs or milled lumber.

BLOCK PLANE

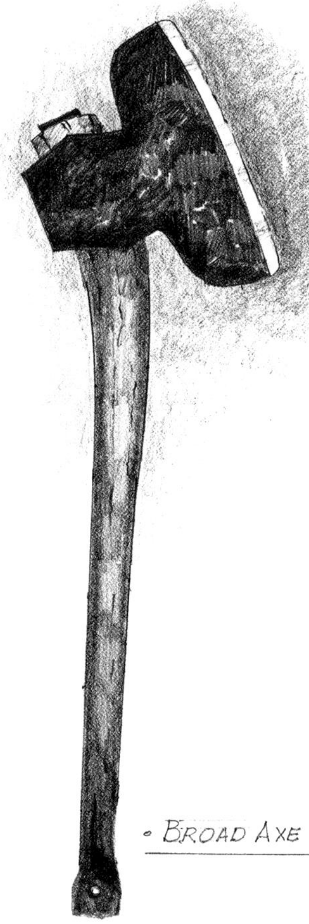

BROAD AXE

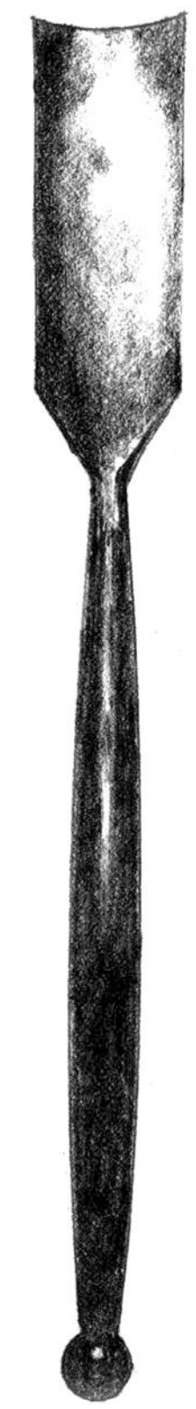

GOUGE CHISEL

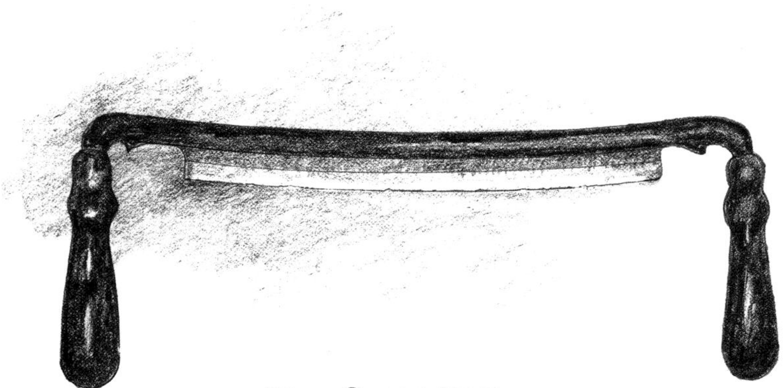

Draw Knife

Turning Saw

Double Screw Clamp

Carpenter's Adze

Log Tongs

Bung Borer

Handscrew

Wooden Screw Clamp

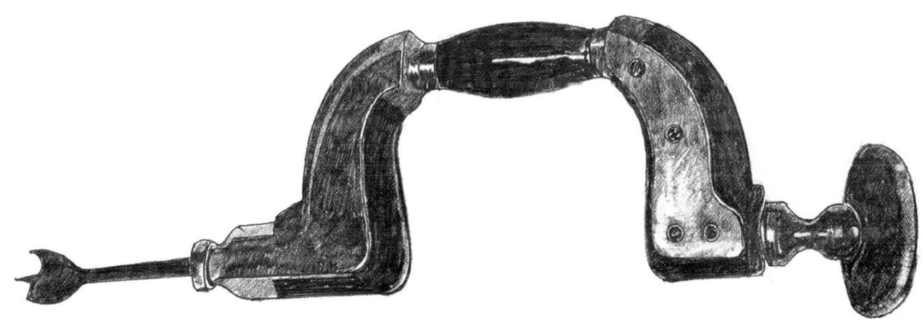

Ebony Ultimatum Brace

A freestanding frame of paired spruce logs supports the porch overhang at Anglers Cabin. It is one of many elegant displays of the log coping skills used to join columns and truss chords on buildings throughout Knapp Ranch.

In Pursuit of Handcrafted Quality

Knapp project superintendent Dennis Thompson of Shaeffer Construction has an extraordinary eye for detail and quality. "My whole career, I've been a builder and I'm very quality-oriented," he says. "The Knapps presented me with the biggest challenge I've ever had, which was to build a house that looks a hundred years old and build it to last another hundred years. That's a tall order. It's a lot harder to do than you'd think."

The challenges inherent in re-creating and re-interpreting history in a building project prompted many conversations between team members and craftspeople. More than once, the desire for authenticity in workmanship was a source of conflict. "Old houses contain a lot of transitional elements because the buildings have settled and moved," says Shaeffer. "Bud didn't want things to look contrived or convoluted, but he wanted to experience as many different building methods as possible." Thompson readily admits that he had difficulty with the idea that rough and unfinished work was acceptable, even desirable, in many cases fretting out loud that the Knapps' determination to make new things look weathered and old was a tough pill to swallow: "I'm a better carpenter than that, and I can make it perfect!" Nowhere is this expectation more evident than in Bud's story about trying to convey the look he wanted in his bathroom: "The woodworker asked me what width I wanted each floor plank to be. I said, 'I don't want you to make them all the same because I don't want that look. I want you to assume that you had to build this floor from a tree that you cut down and you need to make do with every kind of piece that you can get out of the tree.' He got our concept right away, but I had to repeat myself over and over because these guys just couldn't believe that we really meant it. There was no attempt to make a personal creative statement here. We wanted this place to look like it was built by craftspeople. We weren't trying to create a museum, but we purposely wanted to show the value of longevity and how buildings can be designed to last in their environments."

Although the finished product might look rough, it was completed with the utmost pride, care, attention to detail, and quality control. "One of the first criteria, even before we started building the ponds," says Shaeffer, "was to define the edge of the construction zone. We had specific areas where the workers could smoke and eat lunch, and we erected virtually impenetrable fences around each building site. We all understood implicitly that we couldn't re-create this environment, ever." Inside, everything had to be nailed on the backside of the logs or screwed into place. "Bud told me that he didn't want to see a nail that had been puttied over," Shaeffer says, quoting Bud: " 'There will be no exposed nails!' " Everything was finished to this level of detail, even the mechanical rooms. Adds Thompson, "If you want to tell the quality of a house, the first place you should visit is the mechanical room. If it isn't well-done, then you know that's how your rough-in looks. Bud wanted all of the conduit wrapped because he didn't want the mice to eat the wires. At that point in my career, I'd never heard of such a thing!" Shaeffer had to ask a local acquaintance to assist in extending the electric line: "He had a big track hoe with a hydraulic leak out the back. Bud took me aside and said, 'That doesn't cut it here. If he can't clean up his equipment, he shouldn't be here.' "

Betsy Knapp

Builder George Shaeffer adds the finishing touch on a tenon for Marmot Lodge. For thousands of years, craftsmen have used mortise and tenon joints to join together pieces of wood.

Authenticity in Construction

Once the design for the cabins was established, an expert team of custom log home builders, led by Greg Gimbel (Roaring Fork Log Homes) and Roger Sherman (Blue Ox Logcrafters), set up a staging area in an already-disturbed section of Knapp Ranch's lower meadow. With the help of a crew of skilled craftsmen, Gimbel and Sherman transformed architect Gordon Pierce's schematic ideas into a series of structures that showcase traditional log building methods. These handcrafted buildings combine elements of both the rustic Rocky Mountain log cabin style with refined stonework and decorative elements that reflect a northern European influence.

Spruce trees harvested from the nearby national forest were used in the construction of cabin walls. Though they had been standing dead in the forest for over twenty years, their protective bark was still very much intact. No fungus or rot threatened the structural integrity of the wood. More exciting still was the fact that underneath the bark lay a magnificent mosaic in natural hues of gray, bronze, and walnut.

Sherman and Gimbel also made weekend forays to a different forest, returning on Mondays with a truckload of odd-shaped logs and other wood pieces to add to their growing supply of "character logs," which would be incorporated into stair railings, posts, and other architectural details.

The push for authenticity was done for more than merely aesthetic reasons. It was also necessary for the stability and longevity of the buildings, and Sherman and Gimbel were committed to employing authentic joinery and using traditional tools as much as possible. Each member of the crew had a small chainsaw for completing the more delicate inscribe work (fitting the logs together), and a large one for the heavy work (sawing the logs to size and making end cuts). Draw knives, scorps, slicks, and hand adzes—the very tools used in the 1800s to build log cabins—were used to finesse the logs and hide any evidence of saw marks. A band-saw mill was moved onto the property, but often the crew opted to use their chainsaws instead. "Nothing we did here looks like it came out of a magazine," says Sherman proudly, adding, "We freehand flattened most of these logs with a large saw. You can't even tell because, quite simply, that's just how good we are!"

All of the cabins were erected in a staging area on the property, with the logs numbered accordingly. When the team signed off on a structure, the logs would be dismantled, brought to the building site and craned into place. Project superintendent Dennis Thompson and builder George Shaeffer established a zero-clearance policy around each cabin, which meant that nothing would be impacted outside a very tightly contained perimeter. All standing trees were to be preserved. "I kid you not," says Thompson, "we excavated each cabin, put the dirt in a dump truck and stored it on the property with a label on it. When the foundation was completed, we hauled the dirt back to the site it came from. Those cabins look like they have been here for a hundred years because we never introduced any new soils, nor did we destroy any existing vegetation."

Courtesy of Sarah Chase Shaw

Examples of Roger Sherman (standing) and Greg Gimbel's (seated) creative use of oddly shaped wood and character logs are found throughout MacPherson Cabin, where the deck handrails, organic "tree" support column, and interior railings are constructed using unique pieces of wood gathered on weekend collecting trips.

Betsy Knapp

The cabins were first constructed at a staging area in the lower meadow, where they were numbered, then disassembled, and hauled to the cabin site. Here, logs set in a saddle-notch construction start to form the walls of Silver Sal Cabin.

Betsy Knapp

Builder George Shaeffer and crew stand on Silver Sal's foundation. This cabin is a traditional one-room enclosure formed by four log walls joined at the corners, called a single "pen" or "crib." The earliest log cabins were the most likely to be constructed on log pilings or log sleepers, such as those shown in the photo at left, set directly on grade.

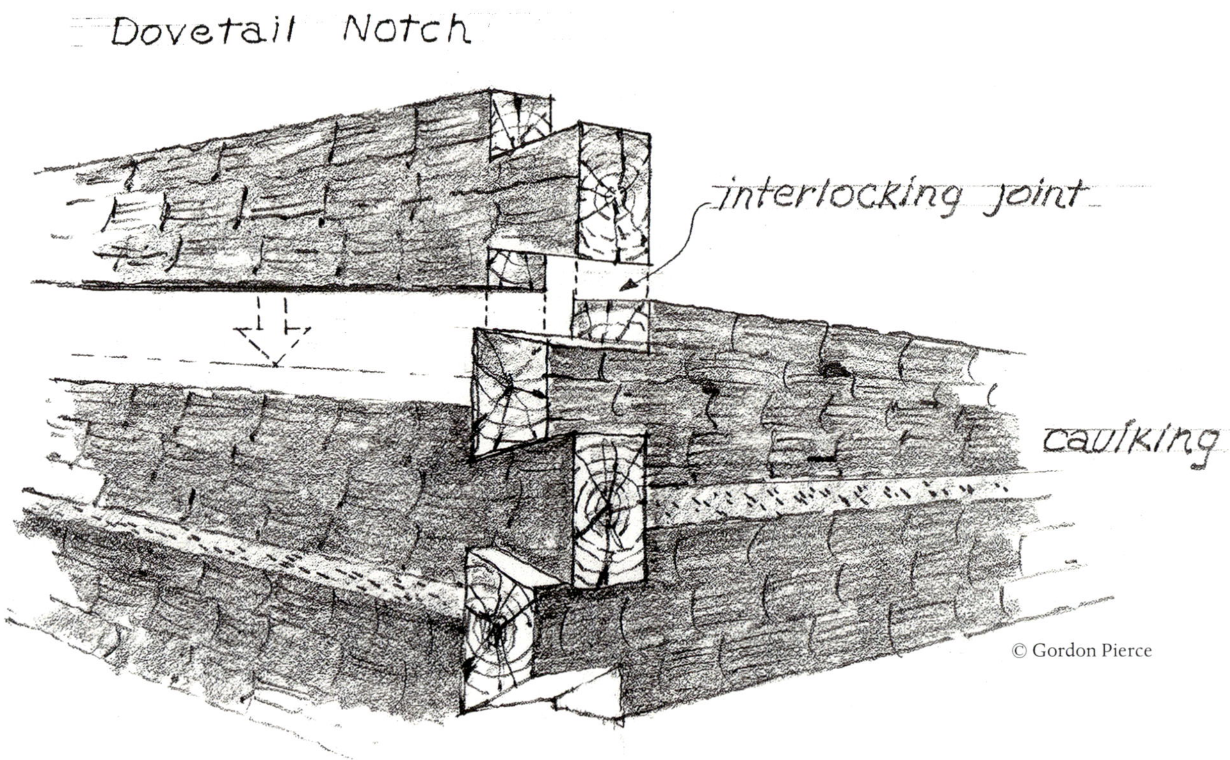

The most advanced and sturdy of the log construction joints, the dovetail notch was used in more sophisticated structures with high, interlocking walls and hewn logs. A home constructed with dovetail notches was a status symbol, a sure sign that a family was prosperous enough to afford more than the crude, round-log cabin of the past.

Knapp Ranch Archives

Property owner Betsy Knapp inspects a mock-up of a full dovetail notch assembly.

Betsy Knapp

Historically, foundation construction was greatly influenced by the climate and the structure's intended permanence. In areas where cabins could sit in deep snow for long periods of time, logs were placed on top of stone foundations to help prevent rotting. At Knapp Ranch, Marmot Lodge's battered foundation is reminiscent of centuries-old alpine chalets, built when mortar was scarce or simply not available, and stone foundations had to be sloped and thickened at the base for increased strength and stability. Deep-set windows ensured a tighter and more insulated interior.

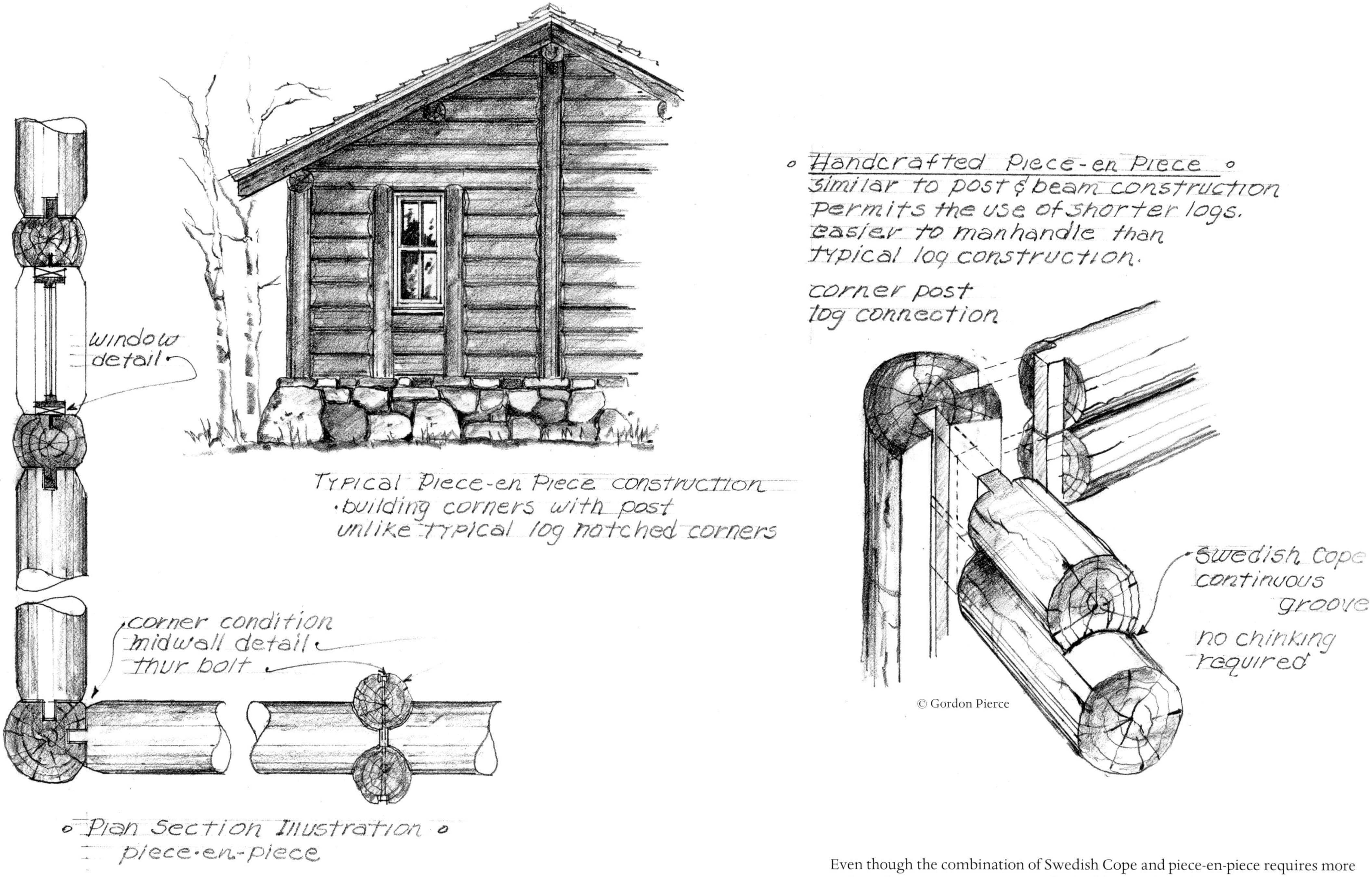

Even though the combination of Swedish Cope and piece-en-piece requires more technical expertise, it was a popular building style with early settlers because it utilized smaller logs, both in length and width, and required no chinking.

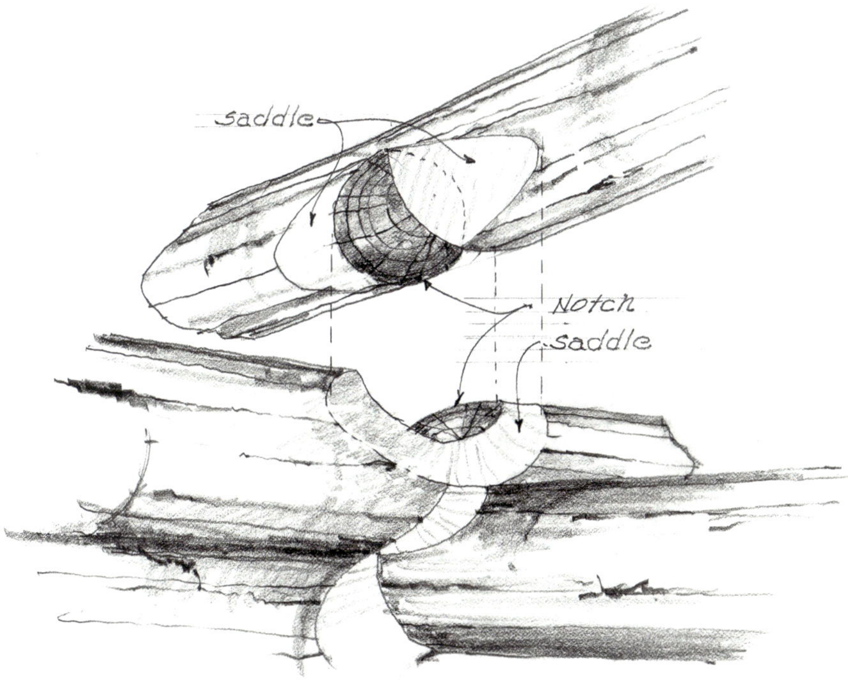

© Gordon Pierce

Saddle notch is typically used with large-diameter round logs. As the logs settle and shrink, the notch seals in place, creating an effective seal against water and cold air.

David Marlow

Logs chopped with a broad ax display "beaver tip" ends, typical of early log cabin construction, where a broad ax was the primary and, in many cases, the only tool available. In saddle-notch construction, log ends are left to project several inches beyond the corner.

Shrinkage and Settlement

"Being versed in proper log techniques and settling issues is so important in log home construction," says Roger Sherman, a Carbondale, Colorado-based builder. "Wood is a natural product, and it changes over time. If you don't accommodate for these changes, your building will slowly fail."

Typically, logs are dried to a 19 percent moisture content and de-barked before using. Leaving bark on a log can encourage insect attack, and it makes scribe-fitting (laying one log seamlessly atop another) more difficult, or even impossible. Using dry timber reduces the amount of settling and shrinkage in a building. Spruce is the predominant species used at Knapp Ranch because, at the time of construction, stands of dead spruce were easy to locate nearby. An added bonus was the fact that these trees, having stood dead for twenty years, were completely dry, bark-free, and had gained a very desirable gray and brown patina.

"Settling" is the term used to describe the loss of wall height over time due to log shrinkage, compression, and slumping. Most builders figure on a 6 percent "settling allowance," particularly for green logs. Dry logs, or buildings with only dovetail notches, may use a settling allowance of less than 6 percent, which is equivalent to three-quarter-inches per foot. The time needed to reach equilibrium moisture content (or complete settlement) depends on a number of technical variables, including wood species, log diameter, initial moisture content, interior temperature, relative humidity, exterior temperature, exposure to sunlight (a factor that is influenced both by depth of roof overhang and exposure), and local climate. Log fibers are cylindrical in shape, with their long axis along the log, and since fibers shrink only in a circular direction, logs generally do not shrink appreciably in length. Logs with a diameter larger than twenty inches can require a longer settling time. Walls in a log home can decrease in height over time as the wood fibers shrink; a nine-foot wall can settle anywhere from one and a half to four inches over time, depending on local conditions.

To allow for such shrinkage and settlement issues, openings called "bucks" are made in log walls. The height of a buck is less than the height of the proposed opening, and the difference in these heights is equal to, or greater than, the settling allowance for the opening. The buck is usually attached to a key—a steel angle iron—that is installed in a vertical slot cut in the log ends of the opening. This key holds the buck in place, effectively restricting horizontal movement of wall logs but allowing for potential vertical settlement. Vertical posts used to support a floor, or roof structure, also require a system that can accommodate settling. At Knapp Ranch, the posts at Marmot Lodge and Anglers Cabin are attached to screw jacks, located at the base of the log. During the first few years after construction, these jacks were adjusted periodically. Now, they are checked annually.

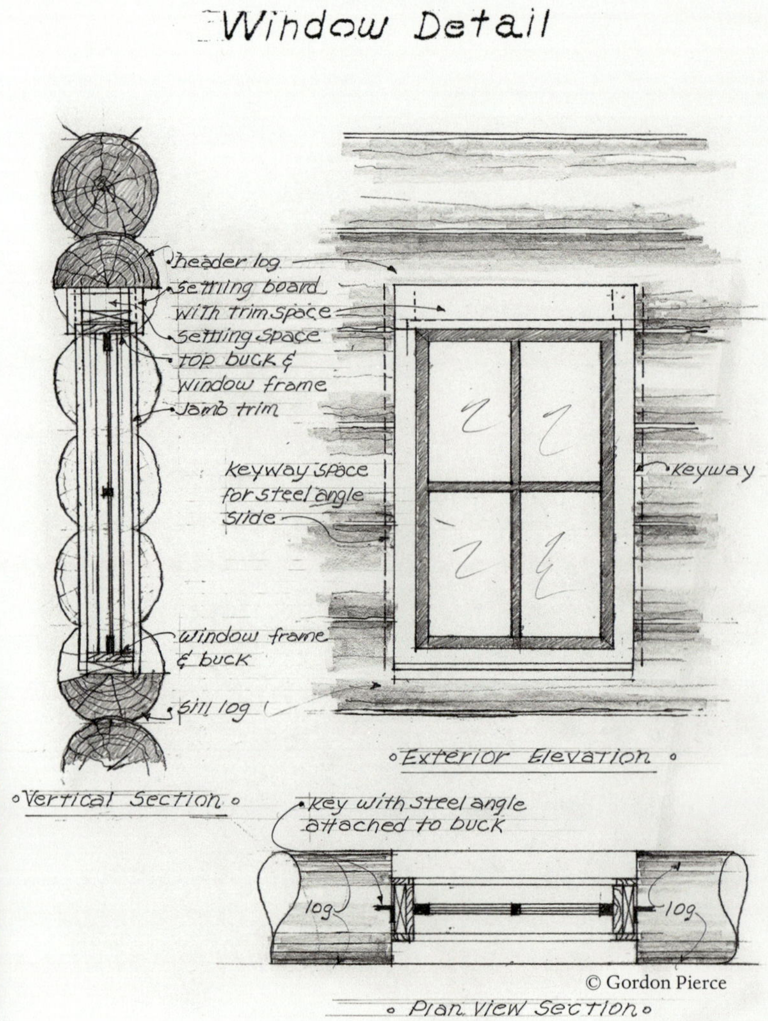

© Gordon Pierce

Above: Log cabin construction is characterized by wood shrinkage, settlement, and movement. A window buck effectively restricts horizontal movement of wall logs, but allows for vertical settlement if necessary. Properly installed, a window buck ensures that the logs above the window do not settle on the frame and distort the opening.

Left: Most of the logs used in the construction of the cabins at Knapp Ranch had been standing dead for almost two decades. As a result, the amount of settling and shrinkage that occurred in the buildings was minimal. Here, a tenon joint of a character post fits seamlessly into a horizontal support beam, allowing for flexibility in the settling of the log wall above the doorway in the Main Lodge.

Betsy Knapp

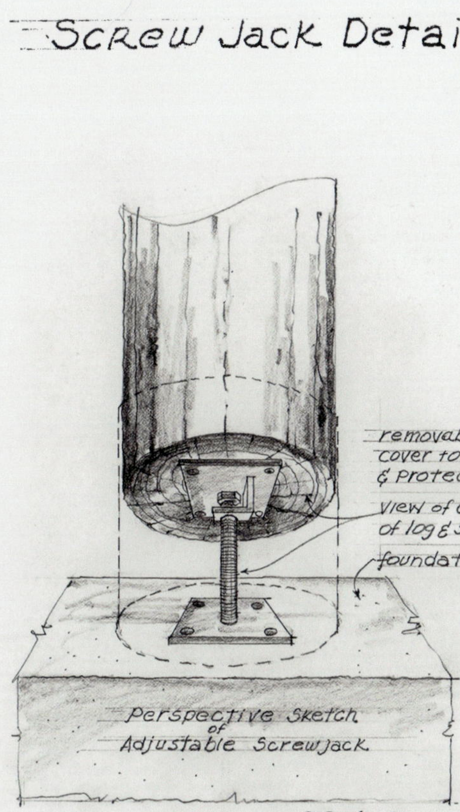

© Gordon Pierce

Windows were installed in a frame, or buck. The bottom buck is fastened to the wall sill log while a settling space is accommodated above the top buck. Rather than attaching the logs to the side sill, the logs are connected to the side bucks by a steel angle which fits snugly into a vertical slot cut into the ends of the wall logs. The wall logs can then move vertically without affecting the window buck.

Wherever wood posts support an upper floor structure or roof, they also must be attached using a system that can accommodate settling. Typically, this is accomplished with screw jacks, which must be adjusted periodically—usually every few months during the first year, and once a year for the next couple of years. This photo, taken during the construction of Marmot Lodge, shows a screw jack installed at the base of a log post in the dining room. The drawing to the right illustrates a screw jack detail.

Knapp Ranch Archives

The entire design and building crew assembled for a photo in front of Marmot Lodge at the topping-off party, September 30, 1995.

The Importance of Site Planning

Some of the decisions, which seemed so intuitive and obvious at the time, would probably raise eyebrows today. So focused was the team on staying true to the character of the story and the place, they deliberately avoided construction choices that might have benefited the long-term maintenance and upkeep of the buildings. For example, even in the arid Colorado climate, moisture can penetrate logs, hastening both fungal and insect attacks. However, hoping to develop a naturally rustic patina on the building exteriors without the use of chemicals, the Knapps decided not to seal any of the logs. This troubled project superintendent Dennis Thompson, a builder whose entire career has focused on quality construction. "When Bud told me he wanted these logs to age naturally, I jumped up and down and demanded that we find a solution we could all agree upon," he says. Instead of sealing the logs, Thompson and the log crew created a muddy concoction of topsoil and water, which they rubbed on the logs to create a weathered earth-tone look. Greg Gimbel and Roger Sherman believe that this technique may have helped protect the logs from the sun and bugs. Keeping the logs dry is always a challenge in this kind of construction. Thompson credits architect Gordon Pierce's deep overhangs—a common feature in northern European mountain architecture—for protecting the integrity of the wood.

"The construction process taught us so much about the integration of basic site planning elements such as sunlight, aspect, slope, topography, views, energy, and insulation with the more cerebral aspects of artistry and craft," says Bud Knapp, adding that they are constantly maintaining and updating the various systems and technologies incorporated in all of the buildings on the ranch. "We have to follow Mother Nature's rules here. If you're not willing to adapt to this type of environment, you probably shouldn't live here."

"The Knapps were able to instill in every one of us who worked on that project a sense of getting the most out of what we have," says landscape architect Rick Lamb. "It wasn't a sense that we were working on a special or privileged project. It was more about how we understand what we have. They didn't want things presented to them in a finished manner. They wanted to know the process. Ultimately, this is what you hope a project will do: Change, evolve and create its own identity over time. The Betsys and Buds of the world hone us and sharpen us. Each one along the way has made us more aware of something than we were before we started."

Betsy Knapp

All of the cabins at Knapp Ranch have sod roofs, a practical roofing technique that originated in northern Europe. Historically, grass and twigs were laid on top of small poles lashed tightly together. Then, six to twelve inches of soil were added, and grass, flowers, and weeds sprouted and grew. As soon as the railroad arrived, however, homesteaders were quick to replace their leaky sod roofs with tarpaper and shingles. In the Rocky Mountain version seen at Knapp Ranch, fresh sod was rolled out onto the roof of each cabin. Given time and adequate moisture, the New World version is nearly indistinguishable from the Old World version.

The following pages contain vignettes of unique architectural details, some of which were specifically designed for a particular cabin, and others that simply sprang from a creative imagination and the willingness to experiment with old-world concepts. In all cases, the use of native materials resulted in random, yet charming, irregularities throughout all of the buildings.

Old-world Craftsmanship in the Twenty-first Century

Learning to do things "the old way" was a challenge for Andy Romero, a lead mason with The Gallegos Corporation in Wolcott, Colorado. Learning how to make the stonework look handcrafted, as if it had been in place for a century, was actually very difficult, says Romero, because "as professionals, we were used to laying things straight and even. Everything here had to look like it had been built by the original homesteader. Once we understood the story and could see how the stone interfaced with the wood, we were able to go with the flow. All the work we did was rustic but clean." For example, the sandstone floor in the bedroom in Marmot Lodge was installed to look as if it had been laid by hand, unprofessionally. That elicited a barrage of comments from the stonemasons, who felt it almost an insult to inlay grout in such a sloppy manner. But when he was asked to make the kitchen fireplace look like the farmer's wife and kids did it in a hurry, Romero, who had never laid a brick in his life, jokes, "I was perfect for the job!"

Rudi Neumayr, an Austrian master wood craftsman, specializes in producing finely crafted, custom interior and exterior architectural woodwork. Evidence of his highly sophisticated and traditional hand work is found throughout each building—in the built-in cabinetry, wall and ceiling panels, staircases, library and the kitchen—and on all the front entry doors. Neumayr, who prefers time-honored methods, says that one of the highlights of working on the Knapps' home was being able to use woodworking techniques from the nineteenth century, because, as he says, everything looked authentic. Neumayr's craftsmanship embodies the concept of sustainability—the sustainability of the final product, and, in the unique quality of expertly crafted wood, the sustainability of the woodworking trade itself. "The work I do is meant to last," Neumayr says simply, "and it's about artistry and an attachment to the material."

Fort Collins-based Point Five Windows, historic window and glass production specialists, conducted detailed research on old cabins in order to provide a product that was historically accurate for each of the log cabins and Main Lodge. Point Five's Randy Helzer describes how the homesteaders would order windows even before they knew the exact dimensions or wall heights of their cabins. If a cabin wall was not as high as originally planned, the homesteader simply adapted: mounting the window horizontally (instead of vertically) in the wall. "We uncovered some of the subtleties of what made things period-correct while working on this project," Helzer says. "We actually built a sliding window, located in the Marmot Lodge kitchen, that looks like a hung window that had been installed on its side. Many windows have actual weights and some have the rope/pulley mechanism, but none of it is functional."

Bob Myers and Stuart Edgerly of Basalt-based Myers and Company, an architectural metals company, worked closely with Associates III to come up with practical solutions for light fixtures that would be authentic to the time period. "We designed everything by hand," says Edgerly, adding that the company was fortunate to have blacksmiths who possessed the intellectual curiosity and metal craft skills to forge beautiful one-of-a-kind fixtures. Myers laments the fact that the American education system has lost sight of the importance of training craftspeople. "Who is going to train the log workers, stonemasons and plumbers of tomorrow? As a society, we should value the skills needed to hone a trade," he says. "The Europeans have mastered that idea, but in this country people who want to work with their hands are a rarity."

"I get excited about craftsmanship and the old ways of doing things," says Bud Knapp. "During my time at *Architectural Digest*, I saw examples of great craftsmanship, and it stayed with me. I came to understand what good quality means. That built a standard in my mind and allowed me to translate to our team what we wanted. We didn't have an end result in mind, but we had a process, and we knew how we were going to get there."

The idea behind the 1930s Works Progress Administration (WPA) and the concept of hiring artists, builders, craftsmen and architects to build bridges, roads, public buildings, and parks all over the country when jobs were scarce (during the Depression) really appealed to me. It was a noble experiment that, to my mind, was very successful. There's a bit of that heritage bug in me that wanted to do somewhat the same thing and I was very proud to give local artists a chance to do exceptional work here. —Bud Knapp

Two distinct stone types—fieldstone on the left and ledger stone on the right—denote the different periods of construction, occurring many years apart, that were described in the fictional design narrative. The boulder on the corner, most likely a glacial erratic found nearby in the forest, was used as a rough quoin accent feature, adding both stability and stylistic whimsy. Stone was used exclusively on MacPherson Cabin's north facade due to the prevalence of snowdrifts, which can extend beyond the roof from January to April.

Shown here is the completed battered foundation and dovetail notch log construction at Marmot Lodge. Window frames set flush with the interior walls result in deep-set windows, an important consideration for insulation and protection in snowy mountain environments.

Clockwise from upper left:
A small window in the garage is framed by a wood header and a sandstone sill.

An arched window is cut out of a protruding stone wall at MacPherson Cabin.

A window is inscribed into the piece-en-piece log construction at Anglers Cabin.

Along the facade of the Main Lodge's carriage house, stonework is purposely altered to suggest that a window was filled in at some point in history.

In nineteenth- and early twentieth-century cabins, windows were cut out in walls and often covered with animal hides or wooden shutters until glass became available. Occasionally, paper greased with animal fat was used to create a translucent, waterproof window covering. Small-paned windows were common due to the fact that, before the railroad, the glass had to be transported by horseback. The windows provided much needed light inside the dark cabins in summer, while their small size guaranteed an insulated and toasty interior during the cold mountain winters. Signed into effect by President Abraham Lincoln in 1862, the Homestead Act facilitated Western migration by offering each settler one hundred sixty acres of public land. The homesteaders had to live on their land for five years before they could receive full ownership. Interestingly, the Homestead Act helped dictate frontier home design and construction, because, in addition to making other improvements to the land, homesteaders had to build a dwelling that was at least ten-by-twelve feet in size, and contained at least one glass window.

Clockwise from upper left: Small windows are set into the raked stone base of Marmot Lodge. The windows at MacPherson Cabin (*top right*) and the Main Lodge (*lower left*), illustrate the progression of skill needed to incorporate window frames into log and stone walls.

David Marlow

Historically, wrought-iron window grills, with their whimsical decorative and regional design influences, were installed primarily to discourage intruders. In the photo on the left, the rippling glass on the front door of Anglers Cabin is protected by a sinuous window grill. A less decorative side entrance to Marmot Lodge is shown in the photo on the right.

David Marlow

The front entrance to the Main Lodge at Knapp Ranch is protected from the elements by a small alcove. The door, handcrafted by designer Rudi Neumayr, is made from red oak, while the exterior columns surrounding it are crafted from local spruce, harvested from standing dead timber in the Flat Tops Wilderness Area above Dotsero, Colorado, with the permission of the U.S. Forest Service. A simple geometric pattern of trusses and rafters complements the hand-forged cylindrical light fixture over the door.

Dutch doors were common in older farm buildings where domestic animals and people often lived in close proximity. With the bottom tightly latched to keep the animals at bay, the top could remain open for use as a pass-through for food, conversation, and ventilation. Shown here is the door connecting the kitchen at Marmot Lodge with the covered porch.

Above: From the porte cochère, a simple barn-wood door set in a sandstone frame marks the side entrance to the Main Lodge. To the right of the door is a hand-forged light fixture encased in amber glass.

Right: Marmot Lodge's vibrant red front door includes a custom sheet-glass inset fabricated by Point Five Windows that captures the look and feel of antique window glass.

David Marlow

David Marlow

David Marlow

Above: Craftsman Rudi Neumayr's design for the door at Silver Sal Cabin includes a specially designed handle meant to resemble a fixture from a historic ship's hold.

Left: The door of MacPherson Cabin features small panes of hand-blown glass that are inlaid between narrow lead mullions in a traditional diamond-shaped design. The Scottish influence is evident in the door's light and colorful design.

Cabin and the Main Lodge doors feature custom hardware designed and crafted by Ken Riley of Roaring Forge in Carbondale, Colorado. Above, the front door to the Main Lodge features a door handle crafted from a tractor knob. At right, handcrafted glass panes provide an impressionistic view of the landscape outside.

Above: Unique iron hinges underscore the substance and craftsmanship embedded in each structure's entry door.

Left: In the absence of metal, a craftsman's solution for a door hinge is a simple yet robust wood strap hinge and pivot.

David Marlow

David Marlow

David Marlow

Light fixtures, designed by the architect and interior designers and created by Myers & Company, are unique to each space. In some cases, larger fixtures are suspended by rustic chains, which allow for a greater diffusion of light. Most fixtures incorporate hand-blown clear or milk glass with visible bubbles.

Clockwise from left:
Porte cochère: Main Lodge
Front Door: MacPherson Cabin
Back Porch: Main Lodge

David Marlow

David Marlow

David Marlow

Clockwise from above:
Front door: Anglers Cabin
Front door: Marmot Lodge
Porte cochère: Main Lodge

Grand fireplaces serve as the focal point for many of the rooms in the Main Lodge and cabins on Knapp Ranch. Designed and scaled appropriately for the space, each fireplace displays a master craftsman's eye and generates a warm and comfortable ambiance.

Left: The fireplace in MacPherson Cabin includes a massive sandstone mantle and much smaller, contrasting ledger stone. Designed largely on site by The Gallegos Corporation's stonemasons, the inset incorporates a keystone arch set in a horizontal dry-stack stone setting. The mantle floats in a field of larger, squared-off rubble stone meant to accentuate the mass of the fireplace. A specially designed iron grate moderates the fire.

David Marlow

Above: A rudimentary keystone arch set in irregular rubble stone, similar to what might have been collected from the surrounding hillsides, is a hallmark of the fireplace in the master bedroom. From the heavy sandstone mantle, the stone face tapers toward the ceiling. A simplistic design compared to the other fireplaces in the Main Lodge, this fireplace would have been the central gathering place for the original settler's cabin.

Left: The refined stonework on the fireplace in the dining room of the Main Lodge reflects a more sophisticated hand, pointing to the influence of European ideas and a skill level that would have evolved over the course of the Main Lodge's expansion. With openings on each side, the fire warms both the dining room and the kitchen. Historically, the raised hearth would have made fire-tending easier on the back and legs. Today, the hearth provides built-in seating on cold winter nights. The low timber-frame ceiling creates an intimate atmosphere of comfort and camaraderie.

Above: The impressive entry hall at Marmot Lodge is embellished with an intricate stair railing made of unique character logs in stick-style patterns.

Right: Split log risers, combined with peeled-log railings fashioned from gnarled character pieces, form a dramatic entry railing at Marmot Lodge. When viewed from afar, these cast-off limbs look as if they are simply a natural extension of the surrounding forest. The newel, or central support pillar of the staircase, is fashioned from a unique character log.

The twisted and irregular deck railing at MacPherson Cabin was meticulously crafted from the branches of juniper trees. Junipers grow at lower elevations, so the homesteader would most likely have gathered the wood from the dry hillsides surrounding a nearby town like Edwards or Wolcott, Colorado.

ESSAY

Sustainability in Craft: Maintaining the Woodworking Tradition

Rudi Neumayr, Aren Design, Inc.
Vail, Colorado

I became an apprentice to a master craftsman in the Tyrolean Alps at the age of fourteen. For three years, I learned all aspects of the woodworking trade. After three years, I became a journeyman, and was given the opportunity to work in different shops to learn the various techniques of the trade. I spent most of my years as a journeyman in a classic specialty workshop for antique furniture restoration and reproductions. Restoring old furniture, or paneling for castles and churches, taught me a lot about handcraft. It was particularly fun when I found markings on hidden joints, left there by the craftsman who made it hundreds of years ago.

I enrolled in the government licensing program and obtained a diploma as a master craftsman, which was a necessary qualification in order for me to open a business. In 1966, I opened my own workshop in a village near Kitzbühel called Brixen im Thale. I left Kitzbühel for New Brunswick, Canada, in 1975 to build a secluded lake house for an Austrian client. I experienced a huge culture shock on that project, partially because my English was rudimentary, but also because I had yet to master the English system of measurement, which was still in place in Canada at the time.

I loved working at a beautiful remote lake in the Canadian woods, but I knew it wasn't the right place for me to grow as a craftsman. A travel agent in New York City told me about the most booming ski resort in the U.S. She said, "Go to Vail!" I went for a scouting trip and found so many Austrians there that I felt right at home. I also learned about the new resort of Beaver Creek, and other developments throughout the Vail and Aspen valleys.

I opened my workshop in Vail in April of 1979 and contacted a few architects in the area. Gordon Pierce was one of the first to connect me with a good clientele for traditional high-end woodwork. From that point on, I was fortunate to work on many projects with Gordon, including the mountain retreat for Bud and Betsy Knapp.

It was very exciting to be involved in a project that entailed such an interesting approach to traditional building methods. This was a project in which quality was expected, but it was also a time for us to apply our creativity in the most personal way. Like craftsmen from another century, we enjoyed the freedom to design all types of woodwork for the home according to our talents and abilities, and then present them for approval. Working with design guidelines and a fictional story developed by the owners, architects and interior designers, we produced doors, paneling and built-ins to fit the story of the home's creation in the 1800s.

Courtesy of Rudi Neumayr

Woodworking is one of the oldest trades in the world, used by almost every civilization to create useful and decorative objects. As with any craft, however, keeping the tradition alive requires sharing and maintaining the knowledge, skill, and techniques used by old masters and contemporary artists. Craftsmanship is a concept of sustainability for the future. If you have a saw, an ax, and the ability to use your hands, you can figure out anything.

The number of traditionally trained wood craftsmen working today is limited to custom woodshops, due in part to the advent of computerized machines and high-tech manufacturing widely available to the furniture and woodworking industry. The wood engineer, or a machinist working in a large industrial furniture factory, must have plenty of woodworking knowledge, but most likely doesn't experience the challenges faced by a craftsman with numerous custom projects. The pressure to complete a project can make an artist forget his craft. A laborer is taught to pay attention to cost and efficiency, but a craftsman labors over details in order to do the job right the first time.

To have an attachment to your material and your trade is one thing; to develop a relationship with your client is quite another, and it's the most important element in good design. If you have a good rapport with your client, you give a bit more. That is the key to success. When you understand the people you're working with, you can create the kind of beauty that only comes about with support for time and process.

An opportunity like this is very rare to find now, because jobs are competitive, and quality is compromised by cost and efficiency. ◻

The Knapp Ranch is not simply shelter: it has a story that considers both the past and the future, and it is based on an overriding respect for and pride of craft and quality execution.

—Rudi Neumayr

Courtesy of Rudi Neumayr

Every visitor reacts differently to this place. Some prefer the Main Lodge because they love a big view of the Rocky Mountains. Others love Silver Sal because they want to feel 'tucked in'. What we created here is based in the learning and the process of creating environments that are true to the evolution of the original settlement pattern of this region. How people experience it is based on their interpretation of this concept.

—Betsy and Bud Knapp

5

FULFILLMENT

INTRODUCING THE BUILT ENVIRONMENT

Settlers in the Mountains

Like the creators of the actual historic buildings that the cabins at Knapp Ranch are modeled after, the architect and design team were highly influenced by both the surrounding environment of the upper West Lake Creek Valley and the tradition of building with locally available natural materials like stone and wood. As the text and images suggest, the design, planning, and care that went into the creation of each building typified both the human settlement patterns and construction techniques of the nineteenth century. They were built to last a hundred years or more by craftsmen whose deep respect for tradition is reflected in their belief that the very act of creating and building something of value takes—and deserves to take—immense time, energy, and thoughtfulness.

Each structure on its own demonstrates the evolution of local methods over several generations. But together, they exude a spiritual and creative sensibility that overrides the architecture. The use of immense logs on relatively small structures reflects the genuine warmth and powerful strength embedded in these buildings. The beauty, simplicity, and elegance of the craftsmanship is awe-inspiring.

The first cabin—"Silver Sal"—is modeled after a rudimentary two-room miner's cabin. In the fictionalized narrative that guided the design of the buildings, it was built quickly in 1869 by a single homesteader using rough rubble stone collected from the surrounding hillsides, and logs cut from the forest. A native of England, this first settler lived alone in the valley for a couple of years, farming the land and grazing a few head of sheep in the open meadows. He wrote to his relatives to tell them about his new life in America, and eventually convinced his brother to join him here. Two years later, his brother and a growing family arrived and built a log cabin next to the lake that now forms one side of the Knapps' Main Lodge.

As more family members arrived from Europe, the compound grew, with each new building reflecting a more sophisticated style than the last, a nod to a growing knowledge and awareness of architectural concepts, and the general improvement of basic construction skills. For example, Anglers Cabin, "built" in 1871, introduces more advanced log construction techniques, including the ability to accommodate multiple doors and windows. Meanwhile, MacPherson Cabin is said to have been built by a Scottish branch of the family in 1877, who introduced a certain vibrancy to the architecture in the form of decorative painting and more colorful interior design. MacPherson is noticeably lighter and airier than the "older" cabins, presumably owing to the combination of log and stone construction, which allowed for the introduction of larger windows.

When the Denver and Rio Grande Railroad reached Edwards in 1887, it brought commerce and industry to the Eagle River Valley, along with more mining to the Lake Creek Valley. It also accelerated the availability and delivery of building materials and interior furnishings. With its deeply set windows, doors and overhangs, Marmot Lodge, allegedly built in 1881, is an amalgam of the design elements from the other cabins. By this time, the settlers had learned how to survive the deep snow and cold temperatures of a Rocky Mountain winter, and their advanced log construction methods, insulation techniques, fireplace design, and window and door design reflected that hard-earned knowledge.

The Main Lodge, too, was expanding to accommodate a growing family, and its carefully planned integration of light and space is reminiscent of an enlightened European design. Heavy timbers support a high ceiling, with windows open to views of the lake and mountains. In a sign of the family's growing prosperity and desire to settle permanently in this valley, the home is surrounded by gardens, both productive and ornamental.

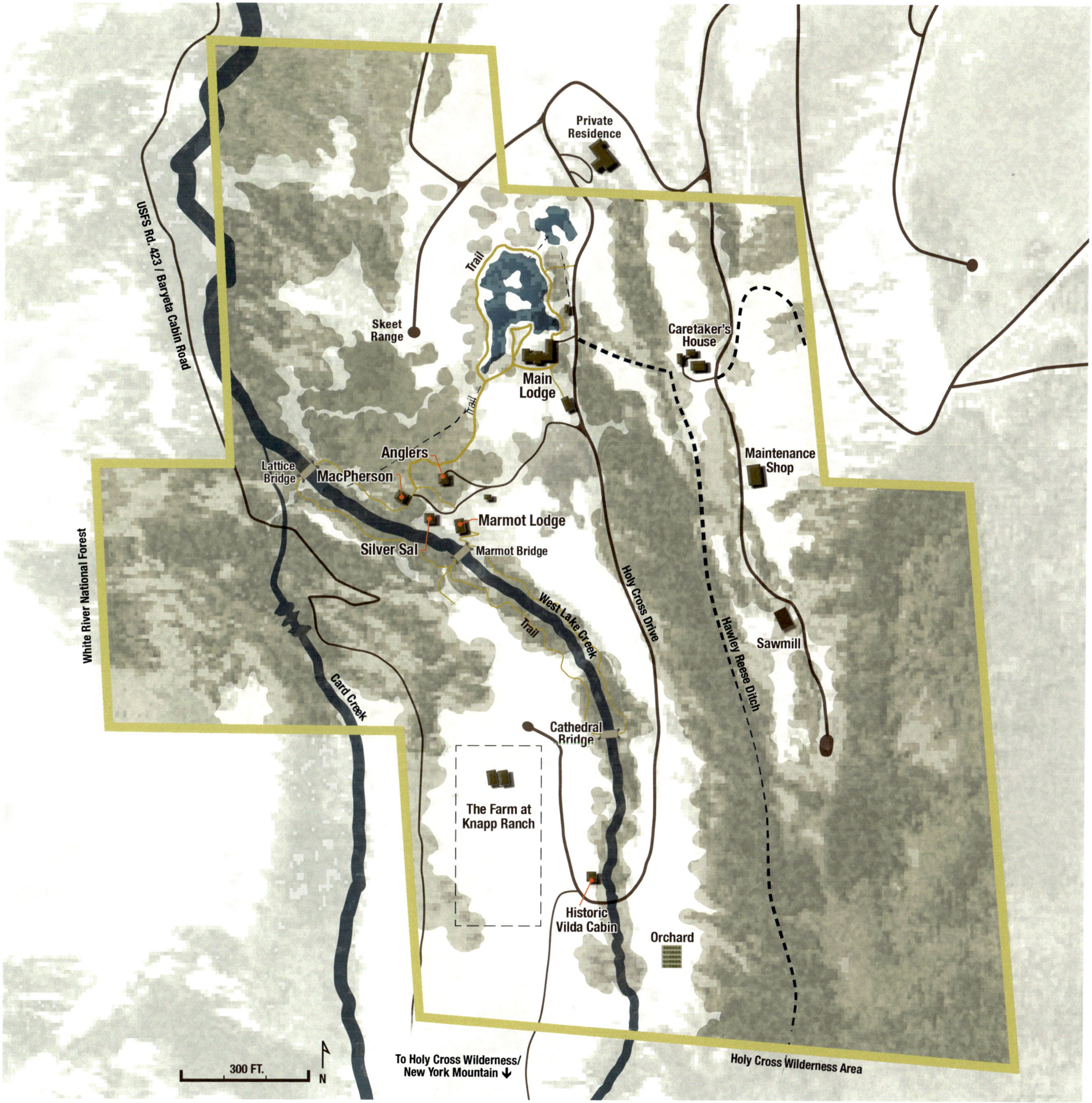

Map by Carly Klein

Opposite: Silver Sal's saddle notch log construction, complete with beaver tip log ends, small windows, deep overhangs and crude stonework is reminiscent of original mining-era cabins in the Rocky Mountains.

Left: Flowing south to north, West Lake Creek bisects Knapp Ranch. The compound of cabins is located closest to the creek, and is connected to the Main Lodge and lake by a series of trails. Holy Cross Drive, the county road, winds along the meadow's edge to the east of the creek. The central growing facilities for The Farm at Knapp Ranch are located at the south end of the property, and the sawmill sits high on the eastern ridge overlooking the valley below.

SILVER SAL
c. 1869

An Authentic Reproduction of an Original Mining Cabin

Perched over the creek and tucked under a protective canopy of mature evergreens, Silver Sal was named for Bud Knapp's intrepid mother, Sarah "Sally" Brasfield. The cabin—with its sod roof, modified one-room enclosure, and saddle-notch log construction—is an authentic reproduction of an original mining cabin. Following the distinctive Rocky Mountain cabin prototype, the front door is located beneath a deep gabled overhang, as a way of adapting to the heavy snowfall in the Rockies. Exaggerated log ends, cut with a broad ax to resemble beaver chew, extend in random widths beyond the cabin walls. Log chinking protects against wind, snow, and rain. A rudimentary fireplace constructed of crude fieldstone is located in one corner. Simple, wide floor planks would have been milled locally from logs harvested in the surrounding forest. Windows, hardware, and other building supplies are small and used only frugally, reflecting the historic fact that in 1869, they could only have been delivered by horseback. The cabin is topped with the kind of sod roof that many early settlers used before the arrival of the train made other roofing materials more easily available. Dug from peat beds located next to the creek, the sod was applied between logs for insulation, or between slats in the roof. Later, other fillers were used to close the gaps (or chinks) between the logs—including straw, paper, cloth, and even dried animal dung. Finally, the insulation was sealed with a layer of mortar, typically composed of clay, mud or dung, and bound with sand, hair, straw, ashes, flour, or sawdust.

Tucked beneath a protective canopy of stately evergreens, Silver Sal's spruce log walls, native stone, and sod roof blend with the natural setting. A screened porch overlooks the steep embankment of West Lake Creek, located directly below. The exterior deck is anchored by newel posts made from robust character logs.

A modest mining cabin, Silver Sal was built by hand, its notches carved with an ax, its logs hoisted atop one another to form the walls of a utilitarian structure.

David Marlow

David Marlow

Above: In the bunkroom, log bunks, appearing as an extension of the surrounding walls, grow organically toward the ceiling.

Left: The cabin's interiors appear almost rudimentary, and yet they are both elegant and comfortable. The simplicity of the time period is noted in the saddle-notch log construction, wide plank floors, and iron and wood furniture. Primary colors brighten the main room, which remains purposely dark due to the small windowpanes and corresponding window frames.

ANGLERS
c. 1871

A "Duplex" Cabin featuring *Piece-en-Piece* Log Construction

Known initially as the "Double Cabin" because of its two separate suites, Anglers would have been built to accommodate an expanded family, presumably related to the original homesteader. It is framed using a traditional Canadian technique introduced by French fur trappers working for the Hudson's Bay Company and known as *piece-en-piece en coulisse*, which, roughly translated, means "to slide one piece on top of another." This technique was popular with early settlers because it employed logs that were both smaller in diameter and shorter in length than those needed to provide structure for long spans. The horizontal infill logs are constructed using the "Swedish Cope" style, a technique in which each log is scribed to the one above in such a way that no chinking is necessary to enforce an airtight seal. The logs are then fitted into grooved supporting vertical posts, placed at the windows, doors, and corners of the cabin. The round sides of the logs face outward, but inside the edges are flat, allowing the interior spaces to be roomier and brighter.

In 1871, windows were still considered a luxury item, installed only when they fit with the limited resources available to early homesteaders. Because most glass was transported by horseback during this time, windows were small, two-foot-by-two-foot squares. In rare instances, two-foot-by-three-foot windows allowed additional light into otherwise dark spaces.

Opposite: Framed by a soft canopy of evergreens and a deep overhang accented by peeled spruce log posts and beams, the front porch of Anglers Cabin provides a comfortable, sheltered space for outdoor living.

Above: Appearing as if it has been there for well over a century, the cabin's log facade and sod roof blend almost seamlessly with the surrounding forest.

David Marlow

Corner windows and stripped, flat logs make for a lighter and brighter interior in the master bedroom, dubbed "The Rainbow Room" in honor of the trout found in West Lake Creek. A custom-designed bed with a hand-painted headboard and a colorful plaid bedding complements the monochromatic texture and color of the interior log work, as well as the wood plank floor.

David Marlow

In "The Brown Palace," named in honor of the famous Denver hotel, twin iron bedsteads are replicas of the type that would have been found in cabins during the late nineteenth century. Fireplaces, located in both bedrooms, provide ambiance and warmth.

MacPHERSON
c. 1877

A Whimsical and Colorful Cabin of Scottish Origin

MacPherson Cabin, named for the Scottish clan on Betsy Knapp's side of the family, displays evidence of a lighter and more sophisticated hand, presumably that of the wealthier European relatives who were lured to the high country of Colorado by the original settler. Constructed to look as if it has emerged organically, even magically, from the ground, the original cabin is a three-level structure with simple saddle-notch log construction and a stone floor. As the family prospered and expanded, they built an additional bedroom wing, connecting it to the main cabin by a hallway with windows, a broom ceiling, and cascading stairs built of a more refined sandstone. Straight lines are anathema to the overall concept, which is best expressed as a subtle integration of natural elements laid in a rustic and creative way. Colorful and light interiors are achieved through an imaginative use of stone with flattened log walls and beams, hand-painted ceilings, doors and cabinets, higher-grade wood floor planks, and hand-troweled finishes. The thistle, an important symbol of Scottish heraldry, appears throughout.

Sophisticated log and stone details include a tapered, dry-stack foundation made of local sandstone interspersed with large boulders. Wood railings are built with specially found character pieces. The roof, whether shaded by the greenery of summer or pillowed by the fluffy snows of winter, disappears magically into the surrounding forest.

David Marlow

Above: Examples of architect Gordon Pierce's unique and fantastical vision are visible throughout MacPherson Cabin. Here, a door opens into a hallway that leads to the hidden bedroom wing. Andy Romero, lead mason for The Gallegos Corporation, recalls how Pierce waved his hands and pointed his fingers, saying, "I want you to create a 'romantic' staircase here. We had never been asked to do that before. I had to tell the mason to build 'romantic stairs': *'Tuve que decirle al albañil que él quería que construyéramos escaleras románticas!'* To this day, we still laugh about it."

Left: Decorative painting is applied to the cabinetry, ceilings, and front door.

David Marlow

The addition of interior color and light are evident in the ornate craftsmanship found throughout MacPherson Cabin. An imaginative use of log joinery and stone detail abound in the living room, including the truly "gutsy" Colorado sandstone mantle.

MARMOT GUEST LODGE c. 1881

Rudimentary Construction Merges with Sophisticated Swedish Style

Marmot Lodge, with its combination of hybrid two-sided log construction and dovetail notch corners, illustrates the transition from rudimentary log cabin construction to a more sophisticated Swedish style in which the logs are shaped to fit on top of each other in an overlapping fashion. Named for the yellow-bellied marmots that inhabit the high mountain meadow and alpine scree fields, Marmot Lodge is the only one of the four guest facilities that includes a kitchen, dining area, laundry, and a central gathering area—complete with a library and television—that is designed to encourage guests to gather for social activities and dining. The Knapps established a tradition of using different locations for meals with their guests, and a typical week might include dinner at the main house on Tuesday, with a big excursion "to town" for dinner on Wednesday. At least one night during the week, guests are encouraged to prepare their own supper at Marmot, following Betsy's desire to create a comfortable and social atmosphere for family, friends, and new acquaintances.

Opposite: Peeled log trusses and beams support a low-pitched gable roof. The front door is sheltered from snow, ice, and falling icicles by the broad overhang.

Above: Marmot Lodge is barely visible in a snow-dusted late autumn landscape.

The covered porch is topped with an open ceiling of timber beams and trusses. The rusticity is reinforced with a specially designed light fixture, peeled log stick-form railings, and Adirondack-style furnishings.

David Marlow

David Marlow

Above: The kitchen, with its broad center sandstone island, high ceiling, and bands of windows, is connected to the porch by a Dutch door.

Left: The living room in Marmot Lodge exemplifies Associates III's ability to transform each room at Knapp Ranch into a warm and inviting space, ideally suited for country-style living. The scale and massing of the living room echoes the majesty of the landscape outside, while wood floors, brightly colored furnishings, and hand-picked lamps and textiles soften its grandeur. Chandeliers in both the living room and kitchen were designed by Associates III and fabricated by Myers & Company.

MAIN LODGE
c. 1873 – 1910

An Aggregation of European and American Log Cabin Architectural Styles

The Main Lodge at Knapp Ranch is an aggregation of architectural styles, designed to reflect the historic influences of the waves of northern European settlers who came to the region. While the widespread use of timber and specific log construction techniques reflect the traditional American log cabin, there is a definite frontier-style sturdiness to this architecture exemplified by the use of stone and large timbers.

From a distance, the style of the home appears unified and complete. It is only upon closer inspection that the period details become apparent, separating the parts from the whole. Says architect Gordon Pierce, "The hand of the architect was never intended to be visible here. Instead, the lodge was supposed to look like it was built by craftsmen over a period of time. It seems so natural and so correct, and the best solution for this property."

In line with the design team's fictional settlement saga, the lodge reflects a number of evolving styles. It begins with a log cabin, (now the master bedroom), and a barn, (now the caretaker's quarters and garage), built in 1873 by the original homesteader's brother, a man with a family, along with a few cows and sheep. Later, as the family grew in size and wealth, they built a typical Colorado farmhouse, filling the space between the two structures with a larger kitchen and dining area. In 1910, inspired by a visit to the grand cathedrals of Europe, they built again, this time connecting the existing structures with an ambitious two-story timber-frame living room space, complete with large picture windows, inglenook fireplace, and formal front door and entry area. Sketches depicting the development of the main lodge can be found on pp. 116-117.

Throughout the lodge, there is a perceptible sense of warmth and protection that emanates from the scale, lighting, use of natural materials, comfortable furnishings, and earth-tone colors mingled with rustic tones of varying shades of red and green. Each room, large or small, is designed to comfortably and flexibly accommodate an intimate gathering of two, as well as a larger group. Doors and windows open to the outside, inviting extended access in the warmer summer months. Inglenook fireplaces, a medieval symbol of hearth and home, occupy a prominent location in the living room and lower level. Also known as chimney corners or "a little room inside a big room," these fireplaces, with their carved benches and handcrafted lighting, are designed to create a sense of sheltering welcome and domestic serenity.

Opposite: Guests enter the Main Lodge compound over a "rumbly-bridge," passing through a rough stone-surfaced tunnel, and emerging into the graveled courtyard where, suddenly, the lake is at eye level with the warm and welcoming living room. Arrival, says architect Gordon Pierce, should feel like "a very subconscious aural adventure. It makes you want to slow down and experience the place."

Above: From across the water, the lake and the Main Lodge appear to merge at eye level, creating an environment that offers intimacy and privacy in a grand and mountainous landscape. High above the valley, No Name Peak glows in the fading sunlight.

To look at the facade of the Main Lodge is to understand the "story" of its development. The garage, with its mottled fieldstone and covered archways, shows the strong influence of eighteenth-century northern European architecture. The combined dovetail-notch and stone construction on the kitchen wing reveals a melding of European and American frontier styles more prevalent in the early 1900s. On the roof, there is a series of peeled logs, cradled in U-shaped supports and embedded in the Italian granite tiles to prevent snow from cascading off the roof.

The beaver-tip ends and saddle-notch log construction are visible on the corner of the master bedroom wing in the Main Lodge. In the fictional narrative that the Knapps and architect Gordon Pierce created to inspire the craftsmen, the first level of this wing is regarded as the original structure built by the homesteader in 1873. The single "pen" (or room) visible in the photo is set on a ledger of rubble stone. A newer wing, added some thirty years later, abuts the log cabin, the influence of an advanced northern European architectural style visible in the more refined stonework, arched windows, and larger windowpanes. The lodge is carefully integrated with the lake and the view, a feature that, combined with a rich display of rusticated details, provides a perfect prototype for mountain design.

Every man should have a place where he can have communion with himself and his surroundings, a personal environment free from disharmony and frustrations: a place to nurture his ideals and aspirations. That place should be his home and if it transcends mere building and comes a work of art it is architecture. —E. Fay Jones, AIA

David Marlow

Above: Layers of hand-adzed square beams frame a view of the dining room from the two-story living room in the Main Lodge at Knapp Ranch. A suspended contemporary wrought-iron light fixture adorned with wildlife and tree silhouettes adds contrast to a nineteenth century Navajo chief's blanket, part of the Knapps' collection of Native American artifacts. The dark wood floors, low timber-frame ceiling, and fireplace render the dining room both more intimate and elegant.

Right: The focal point of the Main Lodge is the two-story, timber-frame living room. Spruce trusses, joined together with specially designed wooden spikes, frame the cathedral-like space of the great room. The mezzanine located on the second floor overlooking the living room is an ideal spot to read, write, or drink tea while observing the changing landscape beyond the windows.

David Marlow

David Marlow

The centerpiece of the kitchen is a large butcher-block island and a brick fireplace, designed to look as if it were built by the original settlers. The hutch, handcrafted by craftsman Rudi Neumayr, features diamond-shaped lead panes and hand-blown glass.

David Marlow

Opposite: Primary colors highlight a handmade Adirondack-style willow bedframe in the master bedroom. The simplicity of the original log cabin construction is evident in the large-diameter peeled spruce logs, timber-frame ceiling joists, wide and irregular plank floors, and rustic furnishings.

David Marlow

The traditional saddle-notch construction and rubble stone fireplace, reminiscent of the original 1870s cabin, complement the vibrant colors of the traditional furnishings in the master bedroom.

David Marlow

Left: Corner windows highlight a claw-foot tub in one of the two master bathrooms.

Opposite: The original homesteader's English roots are evident in the hand-plastered walls, exposed timber frame beams, and window alcoves in the guest bedrooms.

David Marlow

Whimsical ironwork and colored glass add a warm and rustic glow to a light fixture incorporated within the Main Lodge's inglenook fireplace.

A handcrafted bow-tie joint secured with wooden dowels, both functional and decorative in purpose, stabilizes the vertical timbers in the living room of the Main Lodge. The rough texture, visible on the surface of the wood, was created by a hand adze.

We are always in these days endeavoring to separate intellect and manual labor; we want one man to be always thinking, and another to be always working, and we call one a gentleman, and the other an operative; whereas the workman ought often to be thinking, and the thinker often to be working, and both should be gentlemen in the best sense.

— John Ruskin, *On Art and Life*

The vestibule outside the master bedroom in the Main Lodge shows where the original cabin exterior extends into what is now part of the larger main house. The rough-hewn logs—complete with beaver-tip ends that correspond with the era in which it would have been built (1873)—contrast with the more finished siding and woodwork of the hall, designed to look as if it was built some forty years later.

We want to develop a cohesive style among the buildings, as well as the signage, gates, and fences. We envision having a rest hut adjacent to the south side of West Lake Creek that would include a small, enclosed structure for storage of fishing equipment, as well as a porch for lunching or just relaxing and watching the stream go by. —Knapp Property Architectural Program, August 1992

The building compound blends seamlessly into the surrounding environment, a feat that can be primarily attributed to site selection and landscape architecture. Landscape architects Jim Hyatt and Chris Olsen, tasked with building trails, relocating existing boulders, and revegetating the property with native trees, shrubs and forbs, worked closely with the design team to ensure that the sense of authenticity that was so carefully achieved in the architecture translated to everything in the out-of-doors.

One of the major tasks was the realignment of the county road through the meadow below the main house. Slicing into the landscape like a metal straightedge, the existing road had been carelessly bulldozed into place during the fast and furious 1970s, in the period leading up to the proposed Tenderwild development. Taking their cue from the meadow's own rolling topography, Olsen and Hyatt reshaped the road, pulling it closer to the edge of the hill, and planting aspen trees on the downhill side to make it look as if it were winding through an existing grove of trees. "All the answers to everything we did were here on the site, and found in nature. The road was meant to follow the contours more naturally. We were just trying to put nature back," says Hyatt.

Above: A rustic three-rail aspen fence marks the modest two-lane driveway next to Anglers Cabin.

Right: Unobtrusive and carefully crafted wayfinding signs guide visitors at Knapp Ranch.

TO: MARMOT LODGE
CABINS →
WEST LAKE CREEK

The many trails on the property maintain differing widths and surface materials. Here, a narrow gravel path passes through an aspen grove near the Main Lodge.

From the beginning we were clear that we valued effort and premium execution. We weren't inviting people in to tell us what to do, as much as we were encouraging collaboration and participation. The end result is that we have a project with soul. People cared enough to give us their very best. —Betsy Knapp

Beacons of light in a dark forest, lanterns provide just enough illumination to mark the trail without obscuring the crystalline brilliance of the Milky Way overhead.

A trail connecting the Main Lodge and cabins is marked by hand-hewn signs and lanterns. Primary trails throughout the property are covered with mulch from dead pines harvested on the property.

Wildlife and humans share this simple single-track trail, which cuts through the deep grass along the lake's edge.

The walkway connecting Marmot Lodge and Marmot Bridge disappears beneath a pillow of fresh snow.

In midsummer, kids and adults swim, dive, fish, and boat from the lakeside dock. Behind it, a simple shelter offers protection from occasional summer rain showers.

The Main Lodge peeks out from the bright foliage of late autumn.

I have often thought that if heaven had given me choice of my position & calling, it should have been on a rich spot of earth, well watered, and near a good market for the productions of the garden. No occupation is so delightful to me as the culture of the earth, & no culture comparable to that of the garden.

—Thomas Jefferson to Charles Willson Peale, 20 Aug. 1811

6

SUSTAINABILITY

MANAGING THE LAND

Courtesy of Eagle County Historical Society, Eagle Valley Library District

Courtesy of Eagle County Historical Society, Eagle Valley Library District

Previous spread: The lower meadows on Knapp Ranch are cut during midsummer, and bales of nutritious mountain-grown grass hay are sold to neighbors in the West Lake Creek Valley.

Above: Horse-drawn wagons were used to transport lettuce and potatoes to storage sheds along the tracks near the main stations throughout the Eagle River Valley. Here, sacks of potatoes wait to be loaded onto train cars, c. 1910.

Above right: The hot days and cold nights of the high mountain valleys rendered the Eagle River Valley and adjacent areas ideal for growing lettuce. By 1926, approximately two thousand acres of Eagle County were devoted to the cultivation of mountain-head lettuce. In this photo, a group of men and boys take a break while picking lettuce on nearby Bellyache Ridge.

Right: Lettuce was stored in sheds adjacent to the railroad tracks and then loaded onto refrigerated cars kept cool by ice harvested from lakes in the area. From here, the lettuce was shipped to cities in the Northeast, Midwest and South.

Courtesy of Eagle County Historical Society, Eagle Valley Library District

Early Agricultural Endeavors in Lake Creek

Stories of hardy ingenuity and the pioneering spirit of Lake Creek's early homesteaders endure, telling of starry-eyed settlers, some of whom left almost as quickly as they arrived, discouraged by the harsh climate and unfriendly landscape, and others who remained on their land, determined to forge a living in this unforgiving mountain environment. Indeed, historic records include numerous examples of resourceful farming and agricultural endeavors. Almost everyone who chose to settle here turned out to be brave and resourceful, perhaps because they had to be, and they brought with them a certain amount of innovative ideas and entrepreneurial enterprise, as well as a wagonload of tools and a supply of fruit and vegetable seeds.

In the early 1920s, Colorado farmers discovered that lettuce grew deliciously firm and crisp at elevations above seven thousand feet. For a few short years, settlers exploited their land, growing lettuce in many remote mountain valleys, and in the flat open plains along the Eagle and Colorado rivers, creating a kind of "lettuce fever"—a gentler version of the great gold rushes for those settlers who had labored so long and hard to make their lands productive. Wagons transported crates of lettuce to storage sheds located at various points along the railroad line, and ice, cut from the ponds and stored in ice houses along the river, was tossed onto the lettuce, readying it to be shipped out by rail to cities and hotels to the west and the east. At the height of production, several hundred railroad cars of lettuce were shipped every season to points east. Sadly, many of the newly prosperous farmers knew nothing about soil supplements or crop rotation, nor were there any provisions back then for supervised packing or product grading. As a result, lettuce quality declined, and by 1927, only eighteen carloads reached the market. Profits plummeted from $2.50 to fifty cents per crate, and the lettuce boom—a crazy period of quick and easy "green backs"—was over, almost as suddenly as it had begun.

One of the original Lake Creek homesteaders, Joseph Brett, was drawn to Leadville in 1876 by stories of gold and silver. In 1879, realizing that life as a go-for-broke miner in that burgeoning mining town was not for him, he struck out in search of a quieter lifestyle. An account of his arduous journey was found in *A History of Eagle County*, a scrapbook made by high school students in the 1940s:

Joseph Brett and his partner, Mr. J. Bauman, a carpenter, started west early in March with provisions and three pack animals, and running chances of being overcome in a blizzard on the Pass. They had to shovel snow early in the morning until noon, and would then move camp as far as they shoveled snow until the following day. (This routine was repeated daily). It was hard traveling through the snow. It took them thirty-one days to arrive to the present site of Edwards and found the grass growing.[3]

Brett eventually settled at the mouth of Lake Creek on a bluff above the Eagle River. A horticulturalist by training, he set about establishing vegetable and flower gardens, ordering seeds from Denmark, framing hot beds for celery, lettuce, and radishes, planting potatoes and asparagus, and bordering his walls and fences with peonies and roses.

Closer to the ranch, Card Creek, now a pastoral mountain meadow just over the ridge to the west of the Knapps' Main Lodge, was once an active agricultural valley. Melvin Norgaard was a grandson of two Danish immigrants, James and Anna Norgaard, whose family dairy on lower Lake Creek is now a subdivision known as Creamery Ranch. In an interview from 1993 archived at the Eagle County Historical Society, he described the valley and the small cabin hidden in a dense aspen grove on the edge of the meadow.

In the early days, my family lived on the "upper pasture" in the summer, in the homestead cabin next to the huge boulder alongside the road. Near the cabin my dad cleared an area called the "small field," and planted flowers that spelled out EDNA, my mother's name. Big spruces, which held back the water, were abundant in the "small field." In the "big field," dad grew hay. On the west side of Card Creek, he planted loganberries but found it impossible to keep out the deer.

Others, including the homesteader Joseph Vilda, the remains of whose cabin can still be seen at the head of West Lake Creek on Knapp Ranch (see page 82) had small vegetable plots, growing lettuce, radishes, potatoes, rhubarb, and carrots.

Agriculture ... is our wisest pursuit, because it will in the end contribute most to real wealth, good morals & happiness. —Thomas Jefferson to George Washington, 14 Aug. 1787

[3] "Red Book Collection" c. 1943-'47. *A History of Eagle County.* Edwards, CO., Eagle Valley Library District.

Responsible Land Stewardship

"Think globally, act locally" is more than a feel-good mantra shared around the dinner table at Knapp Ranch: It is a guiding principle for the community of artists, academics, business entrepreneurs, and specialists that the Knapps have engaged to think about the future of this place. For over a decade, these people have gathered and shared information, offering big ideas to stimulate awareness and inspire action related to environmental stewardship, land management, and other timely issues. From the thoughtfully designed forest management plan to the collaborative botanic experimentation and research with Wellesley College's "edible landscape" program; from a stringent noxious weed operation to a fisheries habitat management plan; from apiary management to sustainable building practices—every activity on the property is carefully weighed for its environmental, educational, creative, social, and communal impacts.

A commitment to conservation begins with understanding the responsibility that comes with land and water stewardship. The treatment of these resources has unavoidable effects on the downstream user, the nearest neighbors, the small towns and cities that populate the Colorado River corridor, and even users in surrounding states. Sustaining biodiversity through appropriate land and water management is good stewardship, and understanding and anticipating change has become part of the new normal.

The Knapp Ranch of today is a combination of old-world methods and twenty-first-century technology and ideas. It is a hub of learning, creativity, and experimentation, driven by a philosophy of respect and stewardship, and a desire to manage the land for a future that includes the uncertainties of climate change. Accomplishing this mandate requires an intense investment in infrastructure for the future.

"Many people ask us why we put such effort and personal commitment toward the creation of a model of sustainability here," says Bud Knapp, "and it's a question we ask ourselves every day. We chose to live in this remote location. How do we sustain ourselves and our community while maintaining the health and natural beauty of this open land?"

Entrepreneurs by nature, the Knapps believe that they have an opportunity to create an example of world-class production in small-scale agriculture. Like many others, they do not want to rely on acres of corn, grown thousands of miles away, to feed their community. Rather, they want to make their own backyard, whether it's two hundred acres, two and a half acres or a mere two hundred square feet, the ground on which they can rely. "It's about our values and personal preferences, and our interest in linking science with the way we make decisions about the future. It's about considering just how much ecological change we should accept," says Betsy Knapp.

Technology has become a necessary element in the agricultural world, making it easier to manage operations, increase yields, and market products. At Knapp Ranch, weather stations are located throughout the ranch to measure rainfall, temperature, humidity, and wind speed, recording information in hourly increments. This information has already proven useful in understanding the different microclimates that exist on the property, indicating where and which crop cultivation can be most successful, and providing data on the short-term effects of climate change. In the future, the implementation of a system of Quick Read codes will allow for immediate in-the-field access to plant-specific data.

The Knapps plan to continue combining old-world concepts with twenty-first-century technology. "People used to cut down trees to build their homes," says Bud. "They also used to grow food close to homes. Hoping for more efficiency in production, America evolved toward the industrialized mega grid type of life, but it's simply not sustainable for potential growth over the long term. One of several sustainable solutions includes returning to the hearth and growing locally. One hundred years ago, homesteads were sustainable because they had to be. And they were carbon neutral. Today, we want to return to our roots and employ the latest scientific advancements to make greater sustainability possible. We're still homesteaders, but we now have modern technology at our fingertips which allows us—encourages us—to apply science and art to our endeavors." Adds Betsy, "We all have to steward and protect those resources that are vital for growing food. We are now to the point where we should be forging elegant solutions using the combined wisdom of nature and scientific advancements."

The Knapps are also using this property to study the effects of climate change, for even in the upper reaches of the West Lake Creek Valley there is undeniable evidence of a warming world. For example, snow is melting earlier than it did in the last decade of the twentieth century, and temperatures are rising, with the average length of summer "frost-free" periods growing by almost three weeks since 1980. "There's a connectivity to everything around us, and when we ask too much of a limited resource it can disappear," says Betsy. "Our job is to ensure that ideas generated here are made for the greater good—of the community, the region, and the world."

For Colorado, a state that derives roughly 80 percent of its water from annual snowpack[4], a year of low precipitation is always a challenge. Multiply that by two years of below-average rain and snowfall—combined with abnormally high temperatures—and the result is a pattern of dry soils, dry timber, increased chance of wildfire, and the potential for destructive landslides that can damage or destroy water and wastewater treatment facilities, virtually eliminating water supplies.

How will these potentially devastating consequences affect the West Lake Creek and Eagle River watersheds? Linn Brooks, general manager of the Eagle River Water and Sanitation District, says water managers across the region are prepared to prioritize water use and find efficiencies to stretch the supply. Irrigation—of lawns and other non-native plant materials—is now regarded as a low-value use because it consumes the most water and is extremely inefficient. Abandoning a two-hundred-square-foot area of lawn, says Brooks, "could free up enough water to serve a single family home's indoor needs forever. Decreasing outdoor water use is fundamental to future water conservation efforts."

With flexibility and innovation in mind, Knapp Ranch is preparing for the climatic extremes that are likely to occur as a result of climate change by employing the following steps:

Monitoring: Weather stations located throughout the property monitor precipitation and temperature, providing real-time data to scientists studying the effects of climate change in the valley and the larger region.

Water conservation: The lake is more than a major part of the ranch's beauty and ecological vibrancy; it is critical to the ranch's water infrastructure. The lake's storage capacity helps the ranch prepare for year-to-year fluctuations in water availability, and it is also able to provide water for domestic and agricultural use, as well as for fire protection. Future irrigation will rely solely on drip mechanisms in order to reduce soil erosion, evaporation, and nutrient runoff.

Water stewardship: The current Knapp Ranch water mitigation plan returns all but a small portion of water to West Lake Creek, ensuring consistent water availability for downstream users, as well as sustaining the ecological integrity of the riparian and aquatic habitats.

Water quality: Protecting the riparian areas along West Lake Creek is especially important at Knapp Ranch, as their ecological integrity is essential for preventing stream-bank erosion, maintaining cool water temperatures, which in turn moderate the high oxygen content, and maintaining the natural hydrologic cycle that is vital for the aquatic invertebrates and the rest of the aquatic food chain that they support, both on the property and downstream.

Forest agriculture program: Knapp Ranch sells timber through the Forest Ag Program of the Colorado State Forest Service. This program, which offers a tax valuation similar to that given to traditional agricultural lands, was developed to sustain resilient forests that are less vulnerable to insect and disease, and less susceptible to catastrophic wildfire and forest fragmentation. The program also promotes wood products utilization, with participating landowners required to produce tangible items that can be marketed locally or regionally.

Activities such as those outlined above are meant to sustain the ecological integrity of Knapp Ranch into a future that includes climate change. As the struggle to adapt to an increased cycle of extremes in precipitation and temperature becomes one of necessity, not choice, flexibility and innovation—in land and water use and conservation—is key to the property's lasting value well into the future.

Weather stations throughout the property monitor wind, temperature, and precipitation. The data from these stations are used to analyze microclimate patterns and determine various plant habitats and horticultural opportunities. For example, rocks and boulders are natural heat conductors, providing a few degrees of warmth that can extend a bloom season. A line of trees or shrubs can limit the drying effect of sunlight and wind at high altitude, increasing the moisture content of the surrounding soil.

[4] "Colorado River," *Colorado River Water Users Association*, https://www.crwua.org/colorado-river/member-states/colorado.

Professor Kristina Niovi Jones, director of the Wellesley College Botanic Gardens and adjunct assistant professor of Biological Sciences, inspects a young apple tree in the orchard. Jones is working with Knapp Ranch staff to create an edible ecosystem at Knapp Ranch, a challenge at any elevation, but one that is particularly daunting at nine thousand feet. She is confident that the effort will be successful: "We just need to mimic the natural plant communities around us."

Sixty-four fruit trees were planted in the orchard in an ongoing experiment to determine the viability of fruit growing at nine thousand feet. The trees, which include apples, plums, and pears, were selected based on their hardiness and the growers' personal preference. Professor Kristina Niovi Jones and a team of Wellesley College students collect data on an annual basis by monitoring the plants' climatic limits.

Sustainable Agriculture at Nine Thousand Feet

Given the unique conditions at Knapp Ranch, scientists and farmers who are committed to sustainable agriculture have to account for—and balance—many factors. In addition to the basic challenges of soil amendment, crop rotation, soil type, water supply, and elevation, the ranch is home to distinct microclimates, created by protective tree canopies, topographic changes in the landscape, proximity to water, rock outcroppings, and erratic boulders. All of these factors impact the success of farming at this altitude.

"We've learned many lessons over the years about what can and should grow here at nine thousand feet," says Betsy Knapp. "We do not claim to have the answers, but we are always willing to experiment." In marketing The Farm at Knapp Ranch to reflect their commitment to sustainable organic farming, the Knapps insist on monitoring all the agricultural activities that occur on the property and adjusting them on a regular basis to accommodate a variety of agricultural opportunities, as well as the known and unknown effects of a changing climate, including existing water resources, soil composition, and various microclimates.

Knapp Ranch is one of several locations around the country that are participating in an experimental program run by Professor Kristina Niovi Jones and her colleagues at Wellesley College. Called SEED—Science for Edible Ecosystem Design—the program is focused on the study of the biological communities required to support productive agriculture. Near the south end of the property, on a plot of land that was formerly the site of a tree farm, Jones has introduced different varieties of apple, pear, and plum trees into a biological community of complementary plants, including groundcovers, shrubs, and perennials. For fruit trees to be successful here, growers need to pay particular attention to soil nutrients, water, and pest and disease control. Add to that the challenges of harvesting fruit at an elevation of nine thousand feet, and the project becomes even more daunting. Jones is confident she will be able to solve the challenges of growing fruit organically at the ranch. "The idea behind an 'edible ecosystem' garden is a different but complementary approach to organic farming," she says. "Rather than make a traditional agricultural operation more ecologically sound by using organic methods, the edible ecosystem approach mimics a natural ecological system." It's a system she thinks is particularly productive for humans—"although you may still need to outsmart the birds and other creatures also interested in the fruit!"

The key to success is to select species that are well adapted to existing conditions, and also capable of helping the fruit trees to thrive. For example, deep-rooted plants such as comfrey work as elevators for nutrients, bringing phosphorus and potassium from deep in the soil up into their own leaves, which later become nutritious mulch for the tree. Nitrogen-fixing plants like Siberian pea shrub enrich the soil as well. And choosing plants with root structures that are different from those of the fruit trees helps minimize competition for nutrients and water. Non-invasive herbs and other strongly scented plants can serve as "aromatic pest confusers"—discouraging everything from beetles to deer from turning a tree into a meal. Yarrow and coreopsis maintain small flowers over a long blooming season, attracting and retaining beneficial insects in the community. Pollen from native summer wildflowers attracts these insects and bees as well, creating a cycle of diversity that increases the resilience of these ecosystems in the face of the challenges wrought by harsh climatic conditions.

"In our work here, we're basically trying to mimic natural plant communities," Jones says. "Nobody waters and fertilizes plants in the wild. The big difference is that we are extracting the produce from these systems. How do we compensate for that? Permaculture (an approach inspired by the patterns and relationships found in nature) has some answers, as does horticulture. We're using a knowledge-based approach to figure out what works best for this situation, and in the long run, create a series of exportable ideas that can be of use to others undertaking similar activities at high altitude sites throughout the Rocky Mountains."

In addition to the ongoing agricultural research, the ranch grows varieties of vegetables, flowers, and herbs in protected raised beds and gardens, as well as in hoop houses, minimally heated by the sun. Several years of experimentation have reinforced the lessons the early settlers learned the hard way, namely that only certain crops can successfully endure the hot days and cool nights that exist at nine thousand feet. As a result, the gardens are packed with specialty deep green leafy greens, varieties of squash, garlic, onions, leeks, turnips, beets, carrots (atomic red, baby varieties, cosmic purple and Danvers orange), Purple Graffiti cauliflower, Kalettes, Colorado Blue and Red Norland potatoes, and watermelon radishes. Hoop houses and off-site greenhouses are packed with nutritiously dense and flavorful microgreens. In order to provide a substantial and consistent supply of produce to meet the needs of both the local residents and the chefs and restaurants in the Vail Valley markets, the garden areas have been expanded, and plans are underway to include a living laboratory and demonstration space where visiting chefs, farmers, academics, and scientists can share ideas about how to keep a productive farm in balance with this unique environment and physical geography.

When we learned that early settlers grew lettuce, potatoes, and rhubarb in this valley, we became intrigued with the idea that we could do it too. Our integrated collaborative programs increase the role of science and technology to ensure that what we learn here can be useful for others in this field and our place-based systems allow for the development of a longer term perspective and an ability to see how plants, animals and even people interact with this environment over time. In essence, we are working with what nature gives us, recognizing that it will change and being nimble to keep up with it.

—Betsy and Bud Knapp

In the early years, as they were learning what crops could succeed, the Knapps experimented with permaculture in the temporary hoop houses. This sustainable and self-sufficient growing system was built around wide planting beds, vertical plant stacking, rock island mini-microclimates, and transitional edges where different crops blended into one another.

A small kitchen garden located just below the Main Lodge was initially developed to feed both the family and the larger Knapp Ranch community and to provide cut flowers for interior use. Its success over several years encouraged the Knapps to consider expanding their agricultural activities. It is called "Judy's Garden" in honor of Judith Rau, the Knapp's first house manager, an enthusiastic gardener and outdoorswoman, whose idea it was to grow vegetables and cut flowers for the ranch residents.

Developing a productive garden at nine thousand feet takes patience and a willingness to experiment. A short growing season, unpredictable temperatures, and hungry resident wildlife can challenge the mettle of even the most seasoned horticulturalist. However, fertile soil, adequate water, a good fenced area, and nearly constant sun can almost guarantee a bountiful harvest.

Located in the ranch's lower valley, The Farm at Knapp Ranch is a working seasonal farm that honors and preserves the land upon which it is located. The loamy glacial soil combines a healthy balance of silt, sand and clay topped by a layer of rich organic material, ideal for producing fresh and nutritious leafy greens, root vegetables, squash, tomatoes and microgreens. The crops are protected from animal invaders by a twelve-foot-high fence.

Microgreens—tiny edible plants that are more mature than sprouts, but younger than full-grown plants—thrive owing to their quick germination, and are valued for their nutritional value and remarkable flavor. Harvested after the first leaves have developed, they are the smallest of the salad greens and can be grown from almost any plant variety that would produce a mature plant, including beets, radishes, mustard, sunflowers, and even popcorn. The Farm at Knapp Ranch now operates multiple hoop houses—both on the ranch and in Edwards, Colorado—where trays of microgreens are harvested regularly throughout winter and sold to local grocers and restaurants.

Courtesy of Robert Tovias

The Farm grows Colorado Blue Potatoes, or "All Blues," as they are called by the Colorado Certified Potato Association. Prized by chefs for its unusual deep blue color and high nutritional value, the "All Blue" is a particularly thrifty cultivar known for its resistance to disease and hardiness at elevations above seven thousand five hundred feet.

Courtesy of Wendy Rimel

A farm employee uses a two-wheeled walking tractor to harvest potatoes in late August. New potatoes can be harvested when plants begin to flower, approximately eight to ten weeks after planting.

Knapp Ranch Archives

Colorful, eye-catching vegetables are a beautiful and nutritious addition to any meal, and much sought after for use in salad blends. The Farm at Knapp Ranch prides itself on growing hardy and colorful produce, including blue potatoes, atomic red carrots (*at right*), watermelon radish and deep green leafy greens, all of which are popular with local restaurants and consumers. In addition, hardy and disease-resistant vegetables such as these squash varieties (*shown above*) thrive in the high-mountain environment.

Knapp Ranch Archives

Above: Jars of Knapp Ranch native wildflower honey line the shelves at the Edwards' market, Hovey & Harrison. Honey production varies from year to year, owing to environmental factors and hive mortality.

Right: Crates made from beetle-kill pine showcase the variety of vegetables harvested from The Farm at Knapp Ranch. The displays, photographed at The Village Market and Hovey & Harrison (*opposite page*), both in Edwards, Colorado, vary by season. Serving as a reminder for both locals and visitors of the beauty of the Vail Valley, the displays demonstrate The Farm's deep commitment to sustainably produced food.

Protecting the Pollinators

From April to October, bees have free rein to forage for nectar within two miles of their hives. And while other pollinators can be finicky about what they pollinate, bees will pollinate everything. "It's amazing to see how far a bee will fly for good food," says estate manager Carmen Weiland.

At Knapp Ranch, the bees produce an extra-fine grade of wildflower honey derived from a mix of native wildflowers, fruit tree blossoms and annual and perennial flowers planted in garden beds adjacent to the Main Lodge and in The Farm's prolific vegetable rows.

A major challenge for beekeeping in the mountains is protecting the hives from the deep snow and harsh winds of midwinter. "Bees want to eat their own food," say Weiland, "so in the winter we leave them with one hundred pounds of honey, and we only supplement if necessary with sugar patties." For comparison, Weiland says that beekeepers along Denver's less snowy Front Range leave approximately sixty to eighty pounds of honey in their hives. In addition, Knapp Ranch staff wrap each hive, leaving only the entrances open for the bees to take a quick flight during the warm sunny days of mid-February.

Bees are truly some of the hardest-working creatures on the planet, and the services they and other pollinators provide not only help sustain the modern food system but also create attractive habitats for other animals, insects, and birds. At Knapp Ranch, the long-term goal is to use the bees primarily for pollination and honey production, and also to help educate aspiring beekeepers.

Knapp Ranch Archives

The harvest typically occurs at the end of summer, when there is a surplus of one hundred pounds of honey. Here, a beekeeper uses a hot knife to scrape the cells of capped honey from the frame.

A beekeeper clad in protective coverall, gloves, and veil, inspects a frame to determine the health and productivity of the colony. Hives for swarms (or colonies) of bees are stacked on platforms and secured from predators by both a framed structure and an electric fence. In winter, the hives are wrapped to protect the bees from moisture and the cold wind. Only their south-facing entrances remain open, allowing air to circulate within the hive.

Reclaiming the Douglas Fir Forest

In 2008, the mountain pine beetle infestation, well on its way to destroying more than 3.4 million acres of Colorado forestland, was visible in portions of the lodgepole forest on Knapp Ranch. Tinder-dry stands of dead trees and substantial deadfall littered the steep slopes above the valley floor, creating conditions ripe for a catastrophic wildfire.

In response, the Knapps, working with a forest management consultant, prepared a management plan to help guide future forest and wildfire management strategies. One of the objectives outlined in the plan was species diversification within the forest. Although fire likely played a historic role in the spread of the lodgepole and aspen forests on the property, fire in the larger area has been infrequent.

A few charred Douglas fir stumps scattered throughout the property, and one healthy specimen located on a south-facing slope above the sawmill, indicate that at one time these trees supplemented the aspen/lodgepole forest that currently exists. Their absence today, however, can be attributed to the absence of fire, whether man-made or natural. Fire is a major component in the regeneration of Douglas fir forests. Without periodic fires to control lodgepole pine and aspen, their more shade-tolerant and fast-growing competition, young Douglas fir trees, which need sunlight and well-drained soil, are hard-pressed to survive.

In 2014, following the recommendations of the management plan, foresters working at Knapp Ranch initiated a plan to reintroduce Douglas fir throughout the property, using seeds from the one surviving tree on the property. They began by collecting cones in September, when the seeds are firm and brown in color. The cones were spread out to dry on canvas tarps in the maintenance shed. Once dry, their seeds were removed by hand. Then, to encourage germination, a process that normally occurs through fire or extreme heat, foresters froze the seeds for a week. Many of the seeds cracked open, giving them a higher rate of sprouting. The seeds were then planted in a special growing medium and placed in a greenhouse with consistently warm temperatures and a constant light source. Once they had sprouted, seedlings were watered by hand and kept in the greenhouse until they had reached the appropriate size for planting in designated test sites located throughout the forest.

Clearly, this is a long-term experiment, the results of which will not be evident for several decades. The benefits to the surrounding environment are many, and if the project proves successful, it will result in a more ecologically diverse forest that supports not just trees, but a multitude of healthy plants, animals, and micro-organisms.

Forest management efforts include species diversification. The first step in this program is the implementation of a ten-acre clear-cut to encourage natural regeneration and diversification. To aid in the regeneration efforts, ranch employees collect seeds from the only specimens of Douglas fir and Engelmann spruce on the property. The seeds are frozen and thawed several times to facilitate the cracking of the seed coat (a process that mimics the freeze-thaw cycle of a winter season), and then planted in incubation trays. Healthy seedlings are then planted in select areas throughout the forest. Each year, over two hundred seedlings are spot-planted on the ranch. Consistent planting and management should result in the regeneration of a healthy and diverse forest over the next century.

Sustaining Forest Health and Regeneration

After decades of fire suppression and intensive logging, forests throughout much of the Western United States are vulnerable to wildfire and drought. A lack of diversity in species and age class in the forests—the result of the massive clear-cutting that occurred during the late 1800s to support the growth of mining, railroad expansion, and rapid development—further intensifies the situation, rendering the forest more susceptible to widespread mortality from insects and disease.

The Knapps are encouraging research to protect and promote the health and resiliency of the forest and the watershed with the hope of counteracting, and possibly even reversing, the impacts of depleting natural capital, as well as climate change. In conjunction with Colorado's Department of Natural Resources Forestry Division, the ranch is promoting a healthy forest initiative by allocating personnel and infrastructure to assess, plan, execute, monitor, and research practices to restore ecosystem resiliency. A renewable ten-year forest management plan, in place since 2008, was developed to deal with the lodgepole pines affected by mountain pine beetles on the property. Since then, the plan, which is monitored on an annual basis by the Colorado state forester, has advanced to its longer-range objectives of creating and sustaining healthy and vigorous tree stands of varying ages, species, and structural variety. Mini treatments, or small-scale clear-cuts, occur in selective sites throughout the property, measuring between a half-acre to two acres. In these areas, only aspen is removed to allow for the regeneration of a more stable and diverse mixed conifer forest, and to reduce the chance of wildfire. This work is providing scientific data that can be used to evaluate the effectiveness of different forest regeneration treatment methods.

In addition to the efforts underway to maintain healthy tree stands, Knapp Ranch has also implemented its own revegetation strategy in an attempt to add species diversity to the forest. For example, seeds harvested from a single Douglas fir located on the land are propagated and planted throughout the property on an annual basis to replenish this disappearing but resilient tree species.

The lodgepole pine harvested from the ranch has many uses. The bulk of the harvest is milled on site into lumber for retail sale, and for use in building custom furniture. The rest is sold for mulch, veneer, and construction. Beetle-kill lodgepole typically carries with it a recognizable blue stain streaked through parts of the wood fiber, a residual from a fungus deposited by the beetles, and its dramatic natural character enhances the beauty of the tables, benches, chairs, and other furniture that are designed and manufactured at the ranch. As the demand for sustainable and reclaimed wood products increases, the Knapps anticipate being able to produce furniture for use throughout the property, as well as for distribution to interior designers, boutique furniture outlets, and private interests.

We are learning from the land and using its natural capital to steer our operations in a direction that is mutually beneficial, and more importantly, sustains the integrity and the beauty of the natural environment that first attracted us.

—Betsy Knapp

The cut ends of logs show the blue staining characteristic of beetle-kill pine. The mountain pine beetles infect wood with a fungus that leaves behind blue streaks, giving it some appeal for use in trim, decorative panels, and furniture.

The forest surrounding Knapp Ranch was speckled with the skeletons of standing dead lodgepole pine. Under a new forest management plan that recommends specific treatments for each forest type on the ranch, areas that had been significantly affected by the mountain pine beetle epidemic now show an increase in species and age class diversification, while the dead wood has been recycled for use in furniture and other wood products.

The photographs here and on the following two pages illustrate the process used to enhance the mixed-conifer forest, beginning with the selection of individual trees for removal, and ending with the production of milled lumber for sale, or for use in building projects and furniture on the property.

Above: After the trees have been evaluated, loggers use a directional felling technique to avoid, or at least minimize, any damage to younger trees and shrubs in the surrounding forest.

volution did not intend trees to grow singly. Far more than ourselves they are social creatures, and no more natural as isolated specimens than man is as a marooned sailor or hermit.

—John Fowles, *The Tree*

A logger limbs the branches off a Douglas fir, downed in a windstorm. The log will be taken to the sawmill to be debarked and decked with logs of similar size.

Lodgepole pine logs are removed from the forest with a skidder and taken to the sawmill, where they are sorted and decked according to size.

To ensure longevity and diversity, healthy spruce, subalpine fir, and the few Douglas fir that are established in the area are left standing.

Logs are run through the sawmill and cut into board lumber for local distribution and sale. Any remaining odd scraps are chopped into firewood, or used on the property for building projects and furniture.

Helping modern Americans understand and accept the need for human oversight isn't an easy task. It involves reconnecting people to their ecosystems again—getting Americans outdoors and reengaged with the land and the natural world in ways that, to put it bluntly, get dirt under their fingernails, blood on their hands, and even a wood splinter or two in their kneecaps or butts. —Jim Sterba, *Nature Wars*

Furniture, including these Adirondack-style chairs and bench, is made on the ranch using beetle-kill lumber and sold locally.

ESSAY

Nurtured by the Land

Jaymee Squires, Graduate Programs Director,
Walking Mountains Science Center, Avon, Colorado

When biologists try to define the factors that influence the people we become, they talk about the influence of nature versus nurture. We are clearly creatures of both genetics and rearing, but there's a piece that is missing from this dichotomy, and that is the role that landscape plays in our development. Ironically, it's difficult to categorize landscape in this case, for it certainly appeals to that part of us that loves nature, but it also nurtures us, spiritually and physically, shaping the people we become.

I've often wondered if I might be a different person if I had grown up in a different place. I had a mostly idyllic childhood in rural upstate New York, in the area described as the foothills of the Adirondack Mountains, in a neighborhood with streets like Ho Hum Lane, Meditation Way, and Nonchalant Drive. What would I be like if I had grown up in a big city with cars whizzing past my window and cultural opportunities on every corner? Would the part of me that needs open and wild spaces have felt empty, craving something that I didn't even know existed? How does the freedom of open spaces compare to the anonymity of life in a big city? Do city people crave wilderness, or is that need filled by museum exhibits, music, and the diversity of the human race?

We need natural and wild places on a physical level, because they provide clean air, water, and food, but we also need them on a spiritual level. People connect to communities, but they also clearly connect to places, identifying themselves as New Yorkers, Southerners, Midwesterners, and so on. But what makes a place home? We feel more at home in some landscapes than others; like a comfortable pair of jeans, some places are made from just the right materials, with the perfect amount of wear and tear in all the right places, and stains and rips shaped by our stories in them.

It is only recently that I have thought about place as an abstract concept, but I have always been aware of specific places, and how my sanity and wholeness are directly connected to the landscapes around me. The connection of mind to place, in the realm where curiosity meets nature—that is where I have spent much of my personal and professional life. It is my job to teach about science and nature, and how to build connections out of curiosity. And it is in this venue that places like the Knapp Ranch shine through as an example of a place that inspires and enlightens learners of all ages.

The inspiration to live a life shaped by the land around it is a great one, and each time I visit the Knapp Ranch, I feel privileged and awed by its natural diversity and beauty. The last time I was there, I arrived early to prepare for my guided walk. As I followed the trail that zigzagged down to the creek, I greeted the plants like familiar friends, whispering their names: wild rose, raspberry, alder, spruce, and more. I thought about the stories I would tell about each plant, some of them my own, and some borrowed from the lore of others, passed down through books and through story. And later in the day, as I shared my stories about salads made from bluebell leaves and the time I tried to make pancakes out of sorrel seeds, I thought about this place, and all the peoples and animals that had wandered these same trails, and all the stories that it had yet to tell. For while this book shares many stories about this place, the exciting part to me is yet to come. How will the remaining clues to the history of this place reveal themselves and what will they tell us? How will this landscape shape the people who live and grow in it? And how will we steward this place, along with the many others that make up our homes, both near and far, as we move into a new era?

Perhaps one of the biggest questions facing those of us concerned with stewardship of the land is the state of today's youth—the ones to whom we will bequeath our planet. A quick glance at any group of young people usually reveals kids with their attention focused inward on the small screens that seem to consume their very being. If these kids aren't watching the birds, how can we expect them to even notice when one species, and then another and another, goes extinct? In fact, we often cynically assume they wouldn't even notice, at least until it impacts them personally—perhaps not until some recently extinct species is found to be essential to the production of their favorite breakfast cereal, and by then, it's already too late. The damage has been done, and despite intricate technological know-how, it cannot be undone. But this doomsday scenario is not a foregone conclusion; in fact, the seeds of hope are growing within young people everywhere.

As we work as a society to move forward, our goals must become manifold, mirroring the complex ecological cycles and systems that sustain us. We need to practice, problem-solve, and model sustainable and thoughtful solutions to problems big and small. But ultimately, we also need to shape a generation of thinkers with the ability to do what our generation has been unable to do: to live sustainably on planet Earth. If we follow the right models, this path will be one that is much like the trails at Knapp Ranch, traversing a landscape that is lush and diverse, productive and dynamic, lovingly stewarded by those who nurture, and are nurtured by, the land. ◻

Courtesy of Walking Mountains Science Center, Photographer Dominique Taylor

Some varieties of produce, such as lettuces, microgreens and root vegetables, flourish in the fluctuating temperatures and dry air of the upper West Lake Creek Valley. Here, farm manager Sandy Story talks with visitors about the challenges of growing fresh produce at nine thousand feet.

Courtesy of Walking Mountains Science Center, Photographer Dominique Taylor

EPILOGUE
A Vision for the Future of Knapp Ranch

Looking Back to Look Forward

Only fifty years ago, the upper West Lake Creek Valley was home to a handful of homesteads and barns and untouched by growth and development. Fence lines, bowed under the weight of heavy winter snows, delineated public and private lands. Access was limited to the Baryeta Cabin Road—barely visible as it meandered through a dense forest of aspen and spruce, brushing the edge of the open meadows of Card Creek, steepening its pace as it ascended toward the base of New York Mountain.

Forty years ago, ambitious investors laid the groundwork for the development of a subdivision to be called Tenderwild. The Olympic Games of 1976 loomed on the horizon, and Interstate 70 lured ever more tourists into the high country. It looked like yet another cycle of boom and bust would forever transform this pristine mountain valley into a dense subdivision of second homes.

Thirty years ago, the Knapps arrived in West Lake Creek Valley, hoping to find a sense of place in this altogether new and somewhat mysterious mountain landscape. Once they acquired it, their new home—Knapp Ranch—quickly evolved into far more than simply a lovely getaway in the mountains. Instead, it became a place of innovation, creativity and quiet industry, one that was propelled by a vision of preserving the beauty and health of the land, water, and wildlife.

Today, ranch operations and research focus on adaptable and regenerative sustainable farming and land-management technologies related to organic food production, high-altitude ecosystems and water conservation, long-term climate change, best land-use practices, environmental education, and architectural history.

The Knapps' extraordinary journey to understand and develop their relationship to the land and share it with others has touched almost every subject imaginable. This was deliberate, for it was only through thoughtful inquiry that they developed new ideas about influence, opportunity, and appeal. While the end of the journey has yet to be determined, the place itself now has the necessary foundation and infrastructure to develop and sustain a not-for-profit learning center and field station, where think tanks and other organizations can engage in conversation, research, and residency, all with the beautiful central Rocky Mountains as a dramatic backdrop.

The purpose of this book, then, has been to share the journey and to build on the foundation of knowledge gained over decades of experimentation and collaboration. At the end of the day, the conclusion is clear: The Knapp Ranch belongs to a much broader audience, where the exchange of ideas and purpose are key to its legacy.

The Vision

What lies in the future for Knapp Ranch? Ideally, the extraordinary facilities here will be used to support special programs that bring together small and select multidisciplinary groups whose own agendas honor the Knapps' long-term goals—through investments in education, culture and the arts, science and technology, the humanities, sustainable agriculture, and place-based learning. The goal of these retreats will be to come up with new ideas that can directly influence certain fields for the better.

The rustic setting encourages the generation of ideas in a compound of buildings dedicated to the history, conservation, and appreciation of the Rocky Mountain landscape. The property provides multiple opportunities for quiet reflection, social gatherings, retreats, educational seminars, and recreation. Flexible cabin and lodge layouts offer private living and working quarters, while public areas in the Main Lodge and Marmot Lodge are well suited for larger meetings and social functions. Off the ranch, opportunities abound to explore the Vail Valley, an international destination known for its wide range of year-round recreational opportunities, as well as its multiple arts and culture events, and state-of-the-art medical facilities.

The Knapps are committed to the development of a self-sustaining, Colorado-based learning center and field station on the property. The ranch offers opportunities for local nonprofits to host immersive off-site programs and events in natural science, agriculture, and sustainability for both children and adults. In addition, the property is an ideal incubator space in which to research and experiment with promising new alternative energy sources.

At Knapp Ranch, there are excellent opportunities for interdisciplinary scientific research, particularly when it comes to understanding high-altitude ecosystems, and the link between climate science and sustainability, including organic food production, biodiversity and water conservation. As a laboratory for learning about and demonstrating food production at nine thousand feet, The Farm at Knapp Ranch is dedicated to understanding and sharing the benefits of organic farming. As part of the healthy farm-to-table movement, The Farm will provide educational seminars, offer apprenticeships, and educate farmers and others about the benefits of eating with an eye to ecosystem health. As an entrepreneurial business, The Farm will supply fresh and nutritious seasonal produce, honey, eggs, and other agricultural products to regional markets, restaurants, and local chefs.

Members of the Wellesley College Business Leadership Council listen as Dr. Kristina Niovi Jones, director of the Wellesley College Botanic Gardens and adjunct assistant professor of biological science, describes the ways in which regenerative, whole-ecosystem design is being applied to develop solutions that integrate humans with nature and ecological science at Knapp Ranch.

Through an ongoing partnership with the Colorado Division of Forestry, Knapp Ranch will serve as a collaborative research station and forestry sciences laboratory to promote sustainable management of the surrounding forest. Research areas will include fire science, forest and plant health, water and soil management and use, climate change, and human use of the environment. Business opportunities may include the expansion of the wood products using the existing sawmill operation.

Carrying the Vision Forward

From the beginning, passionate curiosity and intelligent observation fueled the Knapps' willingness to experiment and innovate. Knowing that skills and positive results improve with practice, they have been quick to see any failure as an opportunity for improvement. "When you live in a rural location, you have to accept that everything—every plant, animal, rock, and water molecule—was here before you," says Betsy Knapp, "and that every living thing is looking for food at all times. Trial and error have taught us what works and what doesn't." "This environment punishes you if you make a mistake," adds Bud Knapp. "It's like natural selection; it's inevitable."

Given the reality of natural and man-made changes, those contemplating a similar, sustainable future ought to join the Knapps in asking themselves these questions:

- Have we engaged with the landscape in a healthy way, so that our impact has been minimal, and our improvements restorative?
- Are we operating in such a way as to protect in perpetuity this private land so that it may be used for the common good into the future?
- Have we learned from our mistakes?
- Has our intervention had a positive effect on the West Lake Creek Valley and the world beyond?
- Are our activities benefitting the local and perhaps the global community?
- Can we predict the outcome of sustainable agricultural production efforts in light of the effects of climate change?
- Have we led by example and not by doctrine?
- Will our advocacy of clean air, clean water, and open lands inspire and influence the way people think and act about land use?
- And, finally, does this place delight the eye, provide solace to the soul, invite creativity and innovative thinking, and respect the narratives embedded in the landscape in a way that will continue to be valid for decades and centuries to come?

Thoughtful standards like these offer a lens for viewing one's accomplishments as a work in progress, whose details are always subject to adjustment over time. The good work that is being done here is just one example of the many similar efforts occurring around the globe. The results provide examples for what can be done in the future. And the goals are as varied as nature itself.

Will Knapp Ranch offer a perfect model of sustainable and efficient living in an arid, high altitude environment? No. Will everything that happens here reflect a commitment to purism? Not entirely. Is there a constant drive for improvement? Yes. Are our theories being tested and refined? Constantly. Does each new project build upon lessons learned? Absolutely. Knapp Ranch will continue to be a work in progress with a vision meant to be shared. Mistakes, which are sure to happen frequently, can always become opportunities. Successes, rare and fleeting as they may seem, should be documented and appreciated. Both are integral to the base of knowledge being developed on this unique piece of land. It is through the understanding of the interrelatedness of the natural and cultural landscape—and of the people, plants, and animals that live here now, and the future visitors who will tap into the spiritual and inspirational qualities inherent in the place—that it will be possible for us to become better stewards of the land and better problem solvers for generations to come.

The work of Knapp Ranch is only a beginning—a foundation for continuing contributions in design and scientific exploration that others are invited to build upon. Knapp Ranch is dedicated to a philosophy—one that advocates teaching, learning and engaging people to broaden the parameters of their respective areas of interest in a safe, independent and beautiful natural environment.

Nature is not a commodity. It's not something that you can extract whatever you want from and not even try to understand the consequences. Instead, nature is a community of which we are a part and to which we owe our lives. When we cherish nature, we cherish ourselves. When we really appreciate and take care of the natural world, our lives have a meaning that is greater than ourselves and at the same time, essential to ourselves. —John Robbins, Co-Founder of the Food Revolution Network

Visitors pause at the edge of a riparian area along West Lake Creek to learn about the riparian and wetland ecology in Colorado. Though they cover a scant 2 percent of the state, wetlands and riparian areas are considered to be Colorado's most ecologically and economically significant ecosystem. More than 80 percent of wildlife species depend on wetland and riparian areas. In addition, wetlands filter heavy metals, fertilizers and other sediment, provide groundwater recharge, nutrient cycling, carbon sequestration, and stream channel stabilization.

Courtesy of Walking Mountains Science Center, Photographer Dominique Taylor

Experimenting with solar sprint cars, visitors from Walking Mountains Science Center learn how the angle of a solar photo array affects the speed of a car.

Courtesy of Walking Mountains Science Center, Photographer Dominique Taylor

Two workshop participants sample microgreens as they learn about the Knapp Ranch's sustainable agriculture techniques. Growing food from scratch can be a challenge in the mountains, and farm employees continuously monitor the hoophouses to create the perfect environment for their microgreens. Once grown, these tiny vegetables are sold to chefs, markets and restaurants in the Vail Valley, showcasing a true farm-to-table system.

Courtesy of Walking Mountains Science Center, Photographer Dominique Taylor

The ranch is open to people of all ages, giving them a chance to explore nature and perhaps gain a scientific understanding of high-altitude ecosystems and the link between climate science and sustainability—including organic food production, bio-diversity, and water conservation. It provides a perfect opportunity to learn about the wonders of the mountain environment through natural science and sustainability programs. Here, Walking Mountains Science Center founder and vice president Kim Langmaid welcomes guests to the annual Return to Knapp Ranch EdVenture day with a talk highlighting the ranch's sustainable systems.

The ranch's indoor and outdoor spaces can accommodate a variety of special programs and bring together small, select multidisciplinary groups that are willing to honor the Knapps' long-term goals for education, culture and the arts, science and technology, the humanities, sustainable agriculture, and place-based learning.

At Knapp Ranch, people are encouraged to come together to engage in collaborative discussions about big ideas, surrounded by space, beauty and serenity.

How we treat our land, how we build upon it, how we act toward our air and water, will in the long run tell what kind of people we really are.

—Laurance S. Rockefeller

Activities at Knapp Ranch engage and refresh the mind, body, and spirit. Guests can be found exploring by foot and horseback, or skiing on the many trails that wind through the meadows and forest of the upper valley. The lake and creek offer numerous opportunities for fishing, boating, swimming, and exploring. And for those who want nothing more than to listen to the rustle of wind in the trees or the murmur of the creek, there are rocking chairs, benches, and boulders on the porches, along the trails, and overlooking the valley for just such an experience.

AFTERWORD

SARAH CHASE SHAW

TODD WINSLOW PIERCE

The Gift of Awareness

The year 2012 will be remembered as one of the warmest years on record for the contiguous U.S. to date. It was also the year that climate modelers predicted a 10 percent drop in the Colorado River's flow in the next few decades—enough to disrupt age-old water-sharing agreements between farms and cities across the American West. It was during this summer of record-breaking warmth and exceptional dryness across the nation that I became acquainted with Knapp Ranch.

It was a bright and clear day in late June when photographer Todd Pierce and I began exploring the ranch. With cameras and notebook in hand, we set out across the property, bushwhacking our way through thick underbrush, hopping the boulders along the creek, and carefully traversing the ridgelines. Under the mottled canopy of the aspen forest, we stumbled upon patches of early spring wildflowers pushing their way through the thick mat of decaying leaves. Against the base of majestic spruce trees, we discovered foot-deep piles of leftover cones stored there by thrifty squirrels. In the forest and along the stream, we uncovered signs of elk, deer, porcupine, and bear amid the freshly gnawed aspen bark and willow shoots. On the distant ridges, the verdant green of budding aspen leaves marched upward from valley bottom to the peaks above, a sign that, despite all odds, summer would again make its way into the mountains.

At the crest of the hill—no doubt the point where Betsy and Bud Knapp first laid eyes on the valley—a hot wind delivered an acrid smell to our nostrils. In the space of a few hours, this pristine mountain valley had filled with a haze of smoke, blown in from fires as far south as western New Mexico and Colorado Springs. The scent of smoke and the preternatural atmosphere that resulted are memories that will stay with me forever. More importantly, however, the experience opened my eyes to the importance of the work the Knapps are doing to protect this valley from events such as this, and to illuminate the environmental, historical, and cultural importance of the land on which they live. Rooted in their work and their thought processes is an awareness of the need to nourish people, and the desire to steward a lasting sense of place. Even the most casual visitor quickly realizes this; it is rooted in the very heart of this warm and welcoming refuge. And it reaches well beyond the boundaries of the ranch, sharing the many sustainable land-management and agricultural practices that have been implemented here.

Early in our project, Betsy told us that she and Bud wanted to use their property to increase people's awareness of healthy food production and climate change. "The consequence of the interconnectedness of these two concepts affects the way we grow food. That we are able to exist in a place with clean water, clean air, abundant wildlife, and a thriving community is a gift for us, and as a result we are heavily invested in contributing any information we can to supporting a culture of farming and consuming based on a healthy ecosystem," she says.

The Knapps possess, and eagerly share, an extraordinary gift of awareness. This is something that is present in everything they undertake. They pose the questions most of us never think to ask. In one of our early conversations with landscape architect Rick Lamb, he noted that "the Betsys and Buds of the world hone us and sharpen us. They

make us more aware of something than we were before we started, because they want to understand what it is that they have."

What resonates most for me in the Knapps' story is their desire to create a place of lasting quality, soul, and purpose, a place that is rooted in a big idea. In every building, every detail, every living space is a notion that creativity is alive and well, and that its evolution stems from an innate desire to push the limit—to know more. Great places are the result of good ideas carried out with care and stewardship. Knapp Ranch is an example of such a place.

If there is one thing we would like our readers to take away, it is this: Please take a moment to think about how a place like Knapp Ranch appeals to your own aspirations. If you are able to use the information we have shared in these pages in a way that benefits your own personal projects, then we can rest easy, knowing we have done our job.

—Sarah Chase Shaw

Planning, Persistence and Patience

When I was seven years old, my father built me a small log cabin made out of aspen boles in the forest behind our home, just east of Vail. It sat on a gentle slope at the foot of the mountainside, and came complete with a front porch, shingled roof, and small, square windows that allowed me to peek out in all the cardinal directions. From this fort in the woods, I could quietly observe my surroundings and launch explorations along the trails my older brother had created with garden tools he found in the garage. The cabin was just far enough from the house to provide me with a sense of adventure and independence, while not being too far out of earshot of the kitchen window. It was an ideal platform to begin building my own memories and passion for wildness.

My fondest memories all stem from my experiences in nature, whether making quick forays up a neighborhood trail, camping beside glassy alpine lakes, skiing the high couloirs above timberline in early summer, and later, chasing light with a camera and tripod. I've always felt the most alive, present and content while engaged in these activities. Reflecting on the many positive influences that nature has had on my life, I return to my conviction that it is sacred and needs to be protected as much as possible, not just for its intrinsic value but also as a priceless and irreplaceable asset to human beings. Numerous studies have concluded that exposure to nature has a profound and positive effect on our physical, mental and spiritual well-being.

After working in many locations around the country and the world, I've learned firsthand that one of the most effective models of conservation can be found not only within the boundary lines of public lands or national parks, but also within the fence lines of carefully managed private lands. When private land is managed with a sense of reverence and according to sound environmental principles, it can be one of the most effective forms of conservation in the world today.

Within that model of conservation, the Knapp Ranch is a paragon. From the moment Betsy and Bud first set foot on this land, Mother Nature has been guiding them along every step of their journey. The land has always been the inspiration and focal point for every deliberation and decision they've made. Moreover, the Knapps have opened their doors to select educational, research, artistic and intellectual programs and organizations, satisfying the notion that private land ought to be in some way accessible in order to benefit humans as well as wildlife.

When the Knapps first commissioned me to produce a book about the ranch, we had no idea how the project would evolve. What began in their minds as a visual journey across the landscape and through its seasons, weather, and wildlife, evolved into a much more personal, meaningful celebration of their story and their vision for the ranch as a whole. Even though the scope of the original project broadened significantly, my mission remained the same: to artfully and faithfully reveal the spirit of this exquisite place in order to communicate the value of its underlying philosophy of thoughtful stewardship.

I soon realized that in order to be truly successful, I had to do more than simply show what the place looks like: I had to convey what it feels like. As in all my work, truthful documentation and accurate portrayal of nature are sacrosanct. I wanted to capture and preserve all the nuances and subtleties of colors and details so that the viewer can almost feel the temperature of the air and the various textures of grass, stone, wood and water. My favorite images are those that tell a story in a single frame and draw full attention to the beauty of the subject itself so that my viewers forget they are looking at a two-dimensional photograph.

Nearly every visit I made to the ranch yielded a glimpse of wildlife, confirming the fact that this corner of our valley is the preferred habitat for a wide variety of animals. However, I only photographed them if the subject seemed cooperative and if the setting and conditions were favorable. But after numerous fleeting encounters and very little to show for it, it became clear to me that a passive approach wasn't going to cut it.

The first step I took toward obtaining a more intimate view of the animals that live there required the aid of several off-the-shelf trail cameras placed strategically around the property. After only a few weeks, the secret lives of elk, deer, fox, bear and mountain lion were revealed in pale color or infrared images with a digital time stamp. Those grainy vignettes were sometimes haunting, sometimes comical, yet always enchanting and informative. Once behavior and movement patterns began to emerge, I installed high-resolution DSLR camera traps in select areas in order to obtain whisker-sharp images, day or night. Triggered by the breaking of an infrared beam, camera traps are the best way to photograph animals at close range, acting naturally without a human presence. One of the most rewarding captures happened nearly fourteen months after I installed a camera trap along a trail by the creek, when a female mountain lion finally wandered into the frame on an early October morning (see page 53).

In the end, the assignment was a five-year journey of planning, persistence and patience. Many of the images were planned to the last

detail, sometimes months in advance. Others were captured along the way like unexpected gifts. Research and observation lead to educated predictions that in turn lead me to "lucky" moments when everything came together as I had envisioned. Through it all, the love and energy that the Knapps invested into caring for this place only enlivened and propelled my efforts to do it justice, from dark frosty dawns to the last moment of light at the top of New York Mountain.

It was a pleasure and an honor to showcase not only the grandeur and elegance of the natural environment, but also the heartfelt work of designers and craftsmen who, under the spell of this beautiful valley, toiled lovingly over every detail of the built environment. Especially important to me was the opportunity to capture one of my father's most meaningful and memorable architectural projects, to speak for him in a visual way so his original vision could not just be seen, but experienced. That vision, conceived some 25 years ago as he sat by his campfire imagining a story of the first settler to arrive in this valley, has beautifully ripened with nature as he first intended. Applying my artistic skills to capture his was joyful and intuitive.

Exploring every corner of the valley in every season and condition was also essential to my mission as a photographer. For me, photography goes well beyond the ability to simply frame and expose an interesting image. Rather, I believe the photographer is a storyteller and an agent for revealing the things that are most important to us and to our planet. My hope is to instill in my audience a clear and indelible sense of reverence for and a strong desire to protect the natural world. It connects everything, and everyone. Within the covers of this book, my mission was to advocate for a philosophy of thoughtful living and stewardship of the land that can be applied at any scale.

—Todd Winslow Pierce

Betsy and Bud Knapp
Knapp Ranch Archives

CONTRIBUTORS AND ACKNOWLEDGMENTS

Betsy and Bud Knapp

Betsy Wood Knapp was an entrepreneur, angel investor, and philanthropist. She grew up in Evanston, Illinois and, prior to moving to Colorado full-time in 2013, she lived in Boston, New York City and Los Angeles.

Betsy's early career began at MIT, which became the launching pad to her leadership in the computer industry. In the late 1960s, she became a founding member and then president of New York City-based Telmar Communications Corp., a company that pioneered online interactive computer access to consumer behavior databases, and decision support systems for the media and advertising industries. She was responsible for leading the creation of Telmar's operating system and extensive library of interactive software.

After marrying Bud Knapp and moving to Los Angeles in 1979, Betsy became the senior vice president and director of Knapp Communications, the Los Angeles-based owner and publisher of *Architectural Digest*, *Bon Appétit*, and other magazines and books by The Knapp Press, where she was responsible for the company's transition to interactive computer technology and the creation of electronic media products.

In 1986, she founded Wood Knapp & Co. to produce and distribute quality special-interest home video programming, and Wood Knapp Direct, a direct marketer with an annual circulation of five million catalogues. After 1995, following her passion for new business creation, Betsy became actively involved in investing in new technology startups.

Betsy was a founding member of the Committee of 200, a by-invitation association of women entrepreneurs and corporate executives and of the Wellesley College Business Leadership Council. She also was a member of Women Corporate Directors and the International Women's Forum. She was trustee emerita of Wellesley College, where she co-chaired a $400 million comprehensive campaign.

In Los Angeles, Betsy's involvement with UCLA led to her appointment as the first woman to chair the UCLA Foundation, a $1 billion-plus fund which manages private donations for the benefit of the public university. She served on the Board of the UCLA Technology Development Group, which oversees university intellectual property, licensing, and industry-sponsored research. She also served on the Board of Advisors of UCLA Anderson Graduate School of Management.

At Knapp Ranch, Betsy was deeply involved in the development of all aspects of ranch life. She was passionate about learning and practicing best agricultural practices to produce food of superior quality, taste, freshness, and nutrition. Betsy passed away on June 20, 2017.

Cleon T. ("**Bud**") **Knapp**, former chairman and chief executive officer of Knapp Communications Corporation, a company he founded in 1977, is recognized throughout the publishing and business worlds as an innovative, entrepreneurial, and dynamic leader. Knapp Communications Corporation formerly published *Architectural Digest* and *Bon Appétit*, both of which were sold in April 1993 to The Condé Nast Publications, Inc.

Bud entered the publishing industry in the 1950s, working for his grandfather, John C. Brasfield, the founder of *Architectural Digest*. He helped in the office while pursuing studies at the University of California, Los Angeles. Following his grandfather's death in 1965, Bud, at the age of twenty-seven, purchased the John C. Brasfield Publishing Corp. Under his leadership, *Architectural Digest's* mission became one of serving the high-income national consumer market with editorial work dedicated to the concept of the home as a work of art and personal expression.

The success of *Architectural Digest* reaffirmed Bud's contention that, as Americans began to spend more time at home, food and entertaining would become an increasingly important part of creating a fulfilling personal lifestyle. Accordingly, in 1975, Bud's company acquired *Bon Appétit* magazine. Immediately, he instituted major changes aimed at realizing the magazine's potential to meet the growing needs of "food enthusiasts."

In 1977, Bud founded The Knapp Press, a book-publishing subsidiary that has sold 11 million copies, including the bestselling *Italy: The Beautiful Cookbook*. He also established Wilshire Marketing Corporation, a subsidiary that marketed merchandise designed to appeal to the readers of *Architectural Digest* and *Bon Appétit*. That company was renamed "Knapp Communications Corporation" in order to reflect its ownership.

Following the sale of Knapp Communications in 1993, Bud served for ten years as chairman of the Board of Art Center College of Design in Pasadena, and he sat on the Board of Advisors at the UCLA Anderson Graduate School of Management. Currently, he is president of Talwood Corporation, which functions as a family office for administrative, investment and tax planning, and business management activity; and the Knapp Foundation. He has three children—Brian, Aaron, and Laura—and five grandchildren.

The Book Team

Sarah Chase Shaw: Writer and Editor

Freelance writer and landscape architect Sarah Chase Shaw specializes in writing about design and lifestyle in the American West, including landscape architecture, architecture, community planning, environmental design, land use, gardens, people, families, and history. She has authored two books on residential gardens, including *Garden Legacy: the Residential Gardens of Design Workshop*, and *New Gardens of the American West*. A native of Flagstaff, Arizona, and now a resident of Colorado's Roaring Fork Valley, Sarah spends her free time exploring the American West with her husband and son—on foot, in a boat, on a bike, or atop a horse.

Todd Winslow Pierce: Photography

Todd Winslow Pierce is a professional landscape photographer based in Vail, Colorado. His images have appeared in numerous national and regional publications, advertisements, select marketing campaigns, and fine art installations. His commercial and fine art assignments have taken him to locations throughout the U.S., Canada, Europe, Costa Rica, and the Caribbean.

Todd is a lifelong resident of Vail, Colorado, where his father, Gordon, moved in 1962 as a member of the original resort development team. His deep connection to the land, especially to the mountains where he grew up, inspired the consistent focus on landscape and conservation photography that serves as the centerpiece of his work today.

Lisa McGuire: Book Design

Lisa is a graphic designer specializing in exhibit design and book design. She began her career at the Denver Museum of Nature & Science and spent seven years learning her craft while there. Since leaving the museum, she has worked independently designing and producing graphic programs for clients throughout the West.

Lisa's strength is in storytelling. She enjoys working with teams to create strategies that encourage curiosity, enjoyment and exploration, whether by turning pages, or walking through a gallery.

Lisa lives with her husband and various critters in a renovated 1860s cabin at nine thousand feet in the Colorado Rocky Mountains.

Contributing Writers

Kim Langmaid

Kim Langmaid, Ph.D., is the founder, vice president, and director of Sustainability and Stewardship Programs at Walking Mountains Science Center. She has been involved in sustainability, collaborative conservation, environmental education, and nonprofit leadership since the early '90s. In addition to her work at Walking Mountains, Kim teaches in the Sustainability Studies program at Colorado Mountain College, and currently serves on the Vail Town Council. Kim has held positions as the first Colorado program director for the National Forest Foundation; the graduate program director for Teton Science Schools in Jackson Hole, Wyoming; and as a mentor in the Prescott College Master of Arts Program in Environmental Studies and the Ph.D. Program in Sustainability Education. Kim holds a B.S. in biology from Colorado State University, an M. A. in environmental studies from Prescott College in Arizona, and a Ph.D. in environmental studies from Antioch University New England. Kim grew up in Vail and has followed in the footsteps of her parents and grandparents, who were involved in pioneering new initiatives in the early days of the mountain community.

Rick Lamb

Landscape architect Albert "Rick" Lamb has worked on a broad scope of projects throughout the United States, Europe, and the Middle East. Rick's interest in the field of landscape architecture came into focus after a summer spent working with the fledgling Student Conservation Program in Olympic National Park. Rick served on the faculty of Harvard's School of Design and MIT's Center for Real Estate, while working with various offices in Cambridge in Boston. Regular visits with his family in Vail piqued his interest in the landscape of the Rocky Mountains. His firm, Rick Lamb Associates, continues to work on a variety of historic preservation projects in his native Northeast and throughout the country.

Gordon Pierce

Gordon Pierce, founder of Resort Design Associates, came to Vail in the early 1960s from Milwaukee at the behest of his boss and mentor, Fitzhugh Scott—one of the original investors in Vail Associates—to oversee the design and development of the ski resort. From Fitzhugh Scott's simple napkin sketch of Bridge Street, the village took shape, and as Vail grew in both size and importance, so did the number of architectural commissions, leading Pierce to establish his own practice in Vail. In 1997, Gordon, with his son, Andre, opened Resort Design Architects in Avon and San Francisco, focusing on resort design projects in international destinations. Pierce's award-winning projects include the Sonnenalp Resort in Vail, the Grace Bay Club Villas in the Turks and Caicos, the master plans and architectural guidelines for Beaver Creek Village, and the Vidauban Golf and Tennis Resort in Provence, France.

Kari Foster

Kari Foster, owner and principal designer of Associates III Interior Design, is personally and professionally committed to creating healthy, beautiful designs that preserve our environment. As leader of the firm since 1971, Kari works with clients and teams on projects across the globe. Paying attention to detail, listening beyond the words, and using her intuition and design expertise to help owners find their true design voice, Kari has developed long-term, close relationships with her clients. Kari is co-author of the inspiring resource book, *Sustainable Residential Interiors* (Wiley & Sons, 2007, second edition 2014), which earned the Joel Polsky Prize from the ASID Educational Foundation in 2008 for its innovative subject matter.

Rudi Neumayr

Rudi Neumayr began working with wood in 1957 as a young apprentice in Austria. His talent soon led him to work with some of the best architects in Europe, where he honed his craft. He also became recognized by museums and art dealers in Europe for his ability to produce high quality reproductions. After moving to Vail in 1979, Neumayr founded Aren Design, expanding his repertoire into architectural and interior design. His artistic mastery of wood and eye for detail soon became the trademarks of a thriving business.

Jaymee Squires

A native of upstate New York, Jaymee Squires earned a B.A. in environmental science from Binghamton University and a M.S. in education from the University of Phoenix. She also attended Teton Science School's Professional Residency in Environmental Education. Locally, Jaymee has worked as a naturalist for the Vail Nature Center and was one of the first educators at Gore Range Natural Science School (now Walking Mountains Science Center), before she left to teach middle school science at the Eagle County Charter Academy. Jaymee rejoined Walking Mountains in 2009 as the director of graduate programs. She lives in Eagle with her husband and two children, where she enjoys reading, gardening, hiking, camping, canoeing, and making sunshine granola.

Acknowledgments

We would like to thank all those who gave their friendship, time, perspective, and valuable insight to this project.

Linn Brooks, Eagle River Water & Sanitation District, Vail, CO

Steve Cranston, Los Angeles, CA

Larry A. Deckard, AIA, Edwards, CO

Stuart Edgerly, Myers & Company Architectural Metals, Basalt, CO

Kari Foster, Principal, Associates III Interior Design, Denver, CO

Greg Gimbel, Roaring Fork Custom Billiards, Rifle, CO

Randy Helzer, Point Five Windows, Fort Collins, CO

Debbie Hindman, Associates III Interior Design, Denver, CO

Jim Hyatt, (formerly with) EDAW, Denver, CO

Kristina Niovi Jones, Wellesley College Botanic Gardens, Wellesley, MA

Donna Kerwin, Denver, CO

Greg Kerwin, Gibson Dunn, Denver, CO

Aaron Knapp, Redondo Beach, CA

Brian Knapp, Morresville, NC

Laura Knapp, Reseda, CA

Albert R. Lamb, Rick Lamb Associates, Cambridge, MA

George Lamb, Vail CO

Kim Langmaid Ph.D., Walking Mountains Science Center, Avon, CO

Doug Lyle, Left-Hand Excavating, Longmont, CO

Nicole Magistro, The Bookworm, Edwards, CO

Bob Magnuson, Western Bionomics, Steamboat Springs, CO

David Marlow, Aspen, CO

Bob Matsumoto, Los Angeles, CA

Jared McDermott, McDermott Farm and Food Consulting, Glenwood Springs, CO

Jim McHugh, Los Angeles, CA

Bob Myers, Myers & Company Architectural Metals, Basalt, CO

Rudi Neumayr, Aren Design, Vail, CO

Laurie Olin, OLIN, Philadelphia, PA

Chris Olson, (formerly with) EDAW, Denver, CO

Guy Parker, Fruita, CO

Gordon Pierce, AIA, Walnut Creek, CA

Judith & Thomas Rau, Vail, CO

Andy Romero, The Gallegos Corporation, Vail, CO

Tami Schneck, Aquatics Associates, Fort Collins, CO

George Shaeffer, Shaeffer Hyde Construction, Vail, CO

Roger Sherman, Blue Ox Logcrafters, Carbondale, CO

Clifford Simonton, Eagle, CO

Jaci Spuhler, Eagle Valley Library District, Eagle, CO

Annette K. Stelmack, former Design Director, Associates III Interior Design, Denver, CO

Dennis Thompson, Shaeffer Hyde Construction, Vail, CO

Larry Vilda, Lincoln, NE

Les Vilda, Wilber, NE

Susan & Jim Walsh, Stream Team, Longmont, CO

Jamie Werner, Aspen Center for Environmental Studies, Aspen, CO

Shirley Welch, Edwards, CO

Jane Wingfield, Gibson Dunn, Denver, CO

Jean & Jim Wood, Newton, MA

Editors: Jeff Alexander, Hensley Peterson, Carolyn Sackariason, Diane Sylvain

Marketing, Distribution, Production: Douglas Pfeiffer

Advertising and Public Relations: Linda Hill, Hill Aevium

Knapp Ranch Staff, past and present: Kirk Blaine, Natalie Bubalo, Linda Buckley, Connie Bullard, Chris Dellaporta, Aaron Edwards, Tim Galvin, Brian Gandy, Michelle Gennett, Andi Goodrich, Matthew Green, Matthew Heelan, Rita Mary Hennigan, Jim Klatte, Kevin Kottenstette, Julie McElvain, Doran McGuire, Andy McNeill, Pam Miller, Chris Mitchell, David Nally, Seth O'Brien, Ame Onofrey, Wendy Rimel, Davey Salinas, Francisco Santizo, Sandy Story, Karen Tejeda, Claire Thayer, Robert Tovias, Carmen Weiland, and Rebecca Wirth.

Photo Assistants: Jeffrey Hulse, Kate Morris

Reviewers: Colleen Dunn Bates, Doug Graybeal, Nicole Magistro, Rebecca L. Weiss

A train pulls through Pando, near Camp Hale, in mid-winter, c. 1890's.
Courtesy of Eagle County Historical Society, Eagle Valley Library District

END NOTES
INDEX

The following is a small sampling of the resources used in writing this book, which may be of value to those wanting to know more about the subjects covered in it.

1 OBSERVATION

Benedict, Audrey DeLella. *A Sierra Club Naturalist's Guide to The Southern Rockies: The Rocky Mountain Regions of Southern Wyoming, Colorado, and Northern New Mexico.* Sierra Club Books, 1991.

Bird, Isabella L. *A Lady's Life in the Rocky Mountains.* University of Oklahoma Press, 1960.

Crockett, Allen, B. *The Ecology of Colorado.* Self-published, 2014.

Ferguson, Gary. *Rocky Mountain Walks.* Fulcrum Publishing, 1993.

Ferguson, Gary. *The Great Divide.* New York: W.A. Norton, 2004.

Huggins, Janis Lindsey. *Wild at Heart.* Snowmass Village: Town of Snowmass Village, 2004.

Krutch, Joseph Wood. *If You Don't Mind My Saying So ... Essays on Man and Nature.* William Sloane Associates, 1964.

Leopold, Aldo. *Aldo Leopold's Southwest.* Edited by David E. Brown & Neil B. Carmony, University of New Mexico Press, 1995.

Leopold, Aldo. *A Sand County Almanac.* Oxford University Press, 1966.

Mutel, Cornelia Fleisher and John C. Emerick. *From Grassland to Glacier: The Natural History of Colorado and the Surrounding Region.* Johnson Publishing, 1984.

Sibley, George. *Water Wranglers: The 75-Year History of the Colorado River District.* Colorado River District, 2012.

Stegner, Wallace. *The American West as Living Space.* The University of Michigan, 1987.

Zwinger, Ann. *Beyond the Aspen Grove.* The University of Arizona Press, 1970.

For more information about the ecology and geology of the Eagle Valley and the Rocky Mountains, please visit:

Walking Mountains Science Center in Avon, Colorado
https://www.walkingmountains.org

Aspen Center for Environmental Studies in Aspen, Colorado
https://www.aspennature.org

Denver Museum of Nature & Science
https://www.colorado.edu/libraries/libraries/earth-sciences-map-library/map-library-collection

2 DISCOVER

2016 State of the Forest Report for Colorado's Roaring Fork Watershed. Aspen Center for Environmental Studies, 2016.

Athearn, Frederic J. "An Isolated Empire: A History of Northwestern Colorado." *Bureau of Land Management, Colorado Cultural Resources Series, Number Two,* 1982.

Bentz, Barbara. *Bark Beetle Outbreaks in Western North America: Causes and Consequences.* Snowbird, Utah: Bark Beetle Symposium, November 15-18, 2005.

Dorward, Sherry. *Design for Mountain Communities.* Van Nostrand Reinhold, 1990.

Ewing, Clark C., and Margaret C. Ewing. *Early McCoy: A Hundred Year Perspective.* The Print Shop, 1990.

Heicher, Kathy. *Eagle County Characters: Historic Tales of a Colorado Mountain Valley.* The History Press, 2013.

Helphand, Kenneth I. *Colorado: Visions of an American Landscape.* Roberts Rinehart Publishers, 1991.

Loeffler, Jack, and Celestia Loeffler, editors. *Thinking Like a Watershed: Voices from the West.* University of New Mexico Press, 2012.

Marsh, Charles S. *People of the Shining Mountains: The Utes of Colorado.* Pruitt Publishing Company, 1982.

Mehls, Steven F. "The Valley of Opportunity: A History of West-Central Colorado." *Bureau of Land Management, Colorado Cultural Resources Series, Number 12,* 1982.

Noel, Thomas J. *Colorado: A Historical Atlas.* The University of Oklahoma Press, 2015.

Norejko, Richard. "From Metes and Bounds to Grids or a Cliffs Notes History of Land Ownership in the United States." *International Association of Assessing Officers: Fair & Equitable,* (January 2009): 3-16.

Perske, Richard. *Boom Town to Ghost Town: The Story of Fulford.* Eagle County Historical Society, 2015.

Philpott, William. *Vacationland: Tourism and Environment in the Colorado High Country.* University of Washington Press, 2013.

Simonton, June. *Vail: Story of a Colorado Mountain Valley.* Knudson Printing, 1987.

Stone, Tammy. *The Prehistory of Colorado and Adjacent Areas.* The University of Utah Press, 1999.

Waterman, Jonathan and Peter McBride. *The Colorado River: Flowing Through Conflict.* Westcliffe Publishers, 2011.

Williams, Jack E., Dombeck, Michael P., and Christopher A. Wood. *My Healthy Stream: A Handbook for Streamside Owners.* Trout Unlimited and the Aldo Leopold Foundation, 2012.

For more information on the numerous events and vibrant characters that helped shape Colorado's unique history, we recommend the following museums and libraries:

The National Mining Hall of Fame and Museum - Leadville, Colorado
https://www.mininghalloffame.org

The Ute Indian Museum - Montrose, Colorado
https://legacy.historycolorado.org/museums/ute-indian-museum-0

History Colorado Center - Denver, Colorado
https://www.historycolorado.org

The Colorado Ski & Snowboard Hall of Fame - Vail, Colorado
https://www.skimuseum.net

The Map Library Collection at the University of Colorado, Boulder
https://www.colorado.edu/libraries/libraries/earth-sciences-map-library/map-library-collection

The Western History Collection at the Denver Public Library
https://history.denverlibrary.org/western-history-collection

Eagle Valley Historical Society
https://www.eaglecountyhistoricalsociety.com

Eagle Valley Library District
https://www.evld.org/local-history

For more information on water, we recommend these resources:

Colorado Division of Water Resources
https://water.state.co.us

Colorado River Water Users Association
https://www.crwua.org

The Colorado Water Trust
https://www.coloradowatertrust.org

The Colorado River District
https://www.coloradoriverdistrict.org

The Colorado Water Institute at Colorado State University
https://www.cwi.colostate.edu

The State of Colorado Water Conservation Board
https://www.cwcb.state.co.us

Trout Unlimited Colorado
https://www.coloradotu.org

The National Resource Conservation Service
https://www.nrcs.usda.gov

The Colorado Foundation for Water Education
https://www.yourwatercolorado.org

The Citizens Guide to Colorado Water Law, prepared by the Colorado Foundation for Water Education
https://www.colorado.edu/geography/class_homepages/geog_4501_s14/readings/CG-Law2004.pdf

3 METHOD

Barnes, Christine. *Great Lodges of the National Parks*. W.W.West, Inc., 2002.

Bealer, Alex W. *Old Ways of Working Wood: The Techniques & Tools of a Time-Honored Craft*. Castle Books, 1980.

Cammerer, Arno B., Demaray, A.E., Ickes, Harold L., and Wirth, Conrad L. *Park Structures and Facilities*. United States Department of the Interior, National Park Service, 1935.

Chambers, Robert W. *Log Construction Manual*. Deep Stream Press, 2014.

Foster, Kari, Annette Stelmack and Debbie Hindman. *Sustainable Residential Interiors*. John Wiley & Sons, Inc., 2007.

Good, Albert H. *Park and Recreation Structures*. United States Department of the Interior, National Park Service, 1938.

Good, Albert H. *Patterns from the Golden Age of Rustic Design - Park and Recreation Structures from the 1930s* (first edition). Roberts Rinehart, 2003.

Hunt, W. Ben. *How to Build and Furnish a Log Cabin*. Macmillan, 1939.

Kaiser, Harvey H. *Landmarks in the Landscape*. Chronicle Books, 1997.

Kidder, Tracy. *House*. Houghton Mifflin Company, 1985.

Langsner, Drew. *A Logbuilder's Handbook*. Rodale Press, 1982.

McClelland, Linda Flint. *Building the National Parks*. The Johns Hopkins University Press, 1998.

4 ASSEMBLY and 5 FULFILLMENT

McAlester, Virginia Savage. *A Field Guide to American Houses*. New York: Alfred A. Knopf, 1984.

Rybczynski, Witold. *Home: A Short History of an Idea*. Penguin Books USA, 1987.

Rybczynski, Witold. *How Architecture Works: A Humanist's Toolkit*. Farrar, Straus and Giroux, 2013.

Rybczynski, Witold. *Looking Around: A Journey through Architecture*. Viking, 1992.

Rybczynski, Witold. *One Good Turn: A Natural History of the Screwdriver and the Screw*. Scribner, 2000

Rybczynski, Witold. *The Look of Architecture*. Oxford University Press, 2001

Sloan, Eric. *A Museum of Early American Tools*. Funk & Wagnalls, 1964.

Sloan, Eric. *A Reverence for Wood*. Funk & Wagnalls, 1965.

Sloan, Eric. *An Age of Barns: An Illustrated Review of Classic Barn Styles and Construction*. Funk & Wagnalls, 1967.

Wedlick, Dennis. *Designing the Good Home*. Harper Collins Design, 2004.

For more information on the architectural history, we recommend visiting the following museum:

History Colorado Center - Denver, Colorado
https://www.historycolorado.org/adult-visitors/museums-and-historic-sites

6 SUSTAINABILITY

Louv, Richard. *Last Child in the Woods*. Algonquin Books, 2008.

McDonough, William and Michael Braungart. *Cradle to Cradle: Remaking the Way We Make Things*. North Point Press, 2002.

McDonough, William and Michael Braungart. *The Upcycle: Beyond Sustainability - Designing for Abundance*. North Point Press, 2013.

Nash, Roderick Frazier. *Wilderness and the American Mind*. Yale University Press, 1967.

Stern, H. Peter, Peter A. Bienstock, Irving Lavin and Joan Pachner. *Earth, Sky, and Sculpture*. Mountainville, Storm King Art Center, 2000.

Williams, Florence. *The Nature Fix*. W.W. Norton & Company, Inc., 2017.

There are many examples of organizations that share a similar purpose and vision as that of the Knapp Ranch, including:

Stone Barns Center for Food & Agriculture - Pocantico Hills, New York
https://www.stonebarnscenter.org

Shelburne Farms - Shelburne, Vermont
https://www.shelburnefarms.org

Elkstone Farm - Steamboat Springs, Colorado
https://elkstonefarm.com

Colorado Mountain College - Edwards, Colorado
https://coloradomtn.edu/programs/sustainability-studies/mission/

INDEX

Photograph and illustration page numbers are in *italics*.

THE KNAPP PRESS
PO Box 1773
Edwards, CO 81632

Book design by Lisa McGuire.

Distributed by Gibbs Smith
Printing by O' Neil Printing, Inc.
Bindery by Roswell Bookbinding.
Printed and bound in the United States of America.

ISBN: 978-1-4236-5096-6

Library of Congress
Control Number: 2018940280

EARTH, TEACH ME

Earth teach me quiet ~ as the grasses are still with new light.

Earth teach me suffering ~ as old stones suffer with memory.

Earth teach me humility ~ as blossoms are humble with beginning.

Earth teach me caring ~ as mothers nurture their young.

Earth teach me courage ~ as the tree that stands alone.

Earth teach me limitation ~ as the ant that crawls on the ground.

Earth teach me freedom ~ as the eagle that soars in the sky.

Earth teach me acceptance ~ as the leaves that die each fall.

Earth teach me renewal ~ as the seed that rises in the spring.

Earth teach me to forget myself ~ as melted snow forgets its life.

Earth teach me to remember kindness ~ as dry fields weep with rain.

—Ute Prayer